G000129502

15 Days of Prayer
With Saint Dominic

Also in the *15 Days of Prayer* collection:

Saint Teresa of Ávila

The Curé of Ars

Pierre Teilhard de Chardin

Saint Bernard

Saint Augustine

Meister Eckhart

Thomas Merton

Saint Benedict

Charles de Foucauld

Saint Francis de Sales

Johannes Tauler

Saint Louis de Montfort

Don Bosco

Saint Alphonsus Liguori

Saint John of the Cross

Saint Thérèse of Lisieux

Saint Catherine of Siena

Saint Bernadette of Lourdes

Saint Thomas Aquinas

15 DAYS OF PRAYER

WITH

Saint Dominic

ALAIN QUILICI, O.P.

Translated by Victoria Hébert and Denis Sabourin

Liguori
LIGUORI, MISSOURI

Published by Liguori Publications
Liguori, Missouri
www.liguori.org
www.catholicbooksonline.com

This book is a translation of *Prier 15 Jours Avec Saint Dominique*,
published by Nouvelle Cité, 1999, Montrouge, France.

English Translation Copyright 2001 by Liguori Publications.

All rights reserved. No part of this publication may be reproduced, stored
in a retrieval system, or transmitted in any form or by any means—
electronic, mechanical, photocopy, recording, or any other—except for
brief quotations in printed reviews, without the prior permission of the
publishers.

Library of Congress Cataloging-in-Publication Data

Quilici, Alain.
    [Prier 15 Jours avec Saint Dominique. English]
    15 days of prayer with Saint Dominic / Alain Quilici ; translated
by Victoria Hébert and Denis Sabourin.
          p. cm.
    Includes bibliographical references.
    ISBN 0-7648-0716-1 (pbk.)
    1. Dominic, Saint, 1170–1221—Meditations. 2. Spiritual life—
Catholic Church. I. Title: Fifteen days of prayer with Saint Dominic. II.
Title.

BX4700.D7 Q5513 2001
269'.6—dc21   00–066400

Scripture quotations are taken from the *New Revised Standard Version
Bible*, copyright 1989 by the Division of Christian Education of the
National Council of the Churches of Christ in the U.S.A. Used by per-
mission. All rights reserved.

Printed in the United States of America
05 04 03 02 01   5 4 3 2 1
First English Edition 2001

Table of Contents

How to Use This Book

AN OLD CHINESE PROVERB, or at least what I am able to recall of what is supposed to be an old Chinese proverb, goes something like this: "Even a journey of a thousand miles begins with a single step." When you think about it, the truth of the proverb is obvious. It is impossible to begin any project, let alone a journey, without taking the first step. I think it might also be true, although I cannot recall if another Chinese proverb says it, "that the first step is often the hardest." Or, as someone else once observed, "the distance between a thought and the corresponding action needed to implement the idea takes the most energy." I don't know who shared that perception with me but I am certain it was not an old Chinese master!

With this ancient proverbial wisdom, and the not-so-ancient wisdom of an unknown contemporary sage still fresh, we move from proverbs to presumptions. How do these relate to the task before us?

I am presuming that if you are reading this introduction it is because you are contemplating a journey. My presumption is that you are preparing for a spiritual journey and that you have taken at least some of the first steps necessary to prepare for this journey. I also presume, and please excuse me if I am making too many presumptions, that in your preparation for the spiritual journey you have determined that you need a guide.

From deep within the recesses of your deepest self, there was something that called you to consider Saint Dominic as a potential companion. If my presumptions are correct, may I congratulate you on this decision? I think you have made a wise choice, a choice that can be confirmed by yet another source of wisdom, the wisdom that comes from practical experience.

Even an informal poll of experienced travelers will reveal a common opinion; it is very difficult to travel alone. Some might observe that it is even foolish. Still others may be even stronger in their opinion and go so far as to insist that it is necessary to have a guide, especially when you are traveling into uncharted waters and into territory that you have not yet experienced. I am of the personal opinion that a traveling companion is welcome under all circumstances. The thought of traveling alone, to some exciting destination without someone to share the journey with does not capture my imagination or channel my enthusiasm. However, with that being noted, what is simply a matter of preference on the normal journey becomes a matter of necessity when a person embarks on a spiritual journey.

The spiritual journey, which can be the most challenging of all journeys, is experienced best with a guide, a companion, or at the very least, a friend in whom you have placed your trust. This observation is not a preference or an opinion but rather an established spiritual necessity. All of the great saints with whom I am familiar had a spiritual director or a confessor who journeyed with them. Admittedly, at times the saint might well have traveled far beyond the experience of their guide and companion but more often than not they would return to their director and reflect on their experience. Understood in this sense, the director and companion provided a valuable contribution and necessary resource.

When I was learning how to pray (a necessity for anyone who desires to be a full-time and public "religious person"), the community of men that I belong to gave me a great gift. Between my second and third year in college, I was given a one-year sabbatical, with all expenses paid and all of my personal needs met. This period of time was called novitiate. I was officially designated as a novice, a beginner in the spiritual journey, and I was assigned a "master," a person who was willing to lead me. In addition to the master, I was provided with every imaginable book and any other resource that I could possibly need. Even with all that I was provided, I did not learn how to pray because of the books and the unlimited resources, rather it was the master, the companion who was the key to the experience.

One day, after about three months of reading, of quiet and solitude, and of practicing all of the methods and descriptions of prayer that were available to me, the master called. "Put away the books, forget the method, and just listen." We went into a room, became quiet, and tried to recall the presence of God, and then, the master simply prayed out loud and permitted me to listen to his prayer. As he prayed, he revealed his hopes, his dreams, his struggles, his successes, and most of all, his relationship with God. I discovered as I listened that his prayer was deeply intimate but most of all it was self-revealing. As I learned about him, I was led through his life experience to the place where God dwells. At that moment I was able to understand a little bit about what I was supposed to do if I really wanted to pray.

The dynamic of what happened when the master called, invited me to listen, and then revealed his innermost self to me as he communicated with God in prayer, was important. It wasn't so much that the master was trying to reveal to me what needed to be said; he was not inviting me to pray with the same words that he used, but rather that he was trying to bring me to that place within myself where prayer becomes possible. That place, a place of intimacy and of self-awareness, was a necessary stop on the journey and it was a place that I needed to be led to. I could not have easily discovered it on my own.

The purpose of the volume that you hold in your hand is to lead you, over a period of fifteen days or, maybe more realistically, fifteen prayer periods, to a place where prayer is possible. If you already have a regular experience and practice of prayer, perhaps this volume can help lead you to a deeper place, a more intimate relationship with the Lord.

It is important to note that the purpose of this book is not to lead you to a better relationship with Saint Dominic, your spiritual companion. Although your companion will invite you to share some of their deepest and most intimate thoughts, your companion is doing so only to bring you to that place where God dwells. After all, the true measurement of a companion for the journey is that they bring you to the place where you need to be, and then they step back, out of the picture. A guide who brings you to the desired destination and then sticks around is a very unwelcome guest!

Many times I have found myself attracted to a particular idea or method for accomplishing a task, only to discover that what seemed to be inviting and helpful possessed too many details. All of my energy went to the mastery of the details and I soon lost my enthusiasm. In each instance, the book that seemed so promising ended up on my bookshelf, gathering dust. I can assure you, it is not our intention that this book end up in your bookcase, filled with promise, but unable to deliver.

There are three simple rules that need to be followed in order to use this book with a measure of satisfaction.

Place: It is important that you choose a place for reading that provides the necessary atmosphere for reflection and that does not allow for too many distractions. Whatever place you choose needs to be comfortable, have the necessary lighting, and, finally, have a sense of "welcoming" about it. You need to be able to look forward to the experience of the journey. Don't travel steerage if you know you will be more comfortable in first class and if the choice is realistic for you. On the other hand, if first class is a distraction and you feel more comfortable and more yourself in steerage, then it is in steerage that you belong.

My favorite place is an overstuffed and comfortable chair in my bedroom. There is a light over my shoulder, and the chair reclines if I feel a need to recline. Once in a while, I get lucky and the sun comes through my window and bathes the entire room in light. I have other options and other places that are available to me but this is the place that I prefer.

Time: Choose a time during the day when you are most alert and when you are most receptive to reflection, meditation, and prayer. The time that you choose is an essential component. If you are a morning person, for example, you should choose a time that is in the morning. If you are more alert in the afternoon, choose an afternoon time slot; and if evening is your preference, then by all means choose the evening. Try to avoid "peak" periods in your daily routine when you know that you might be disturbed. The time that you choose needs to be your time and needs to work for you.

It is also important that you choose how much time you

will spend with your companion each day. For some it will be possible to set aside enough time in order to read and reflect on all the material that is offered for a given day. For others, it might not be possible to devote one time to the suggested material for the day, so the prayer period may need to be extended for two, three, or even more sessions. It is not important how long it takes you; it is only important that it works for you and that you remain committed to that which is possible.

For myself I have found that fifteen minutes in the early morning, while I am still in my robe and pajamas and before my morning coffee, and even before I prepare myself for the day, is the best time. No one expects to see me or to interact with me because I have not yet "announced" the fact that I am awake or even on the move. However, once someone hears me in the bathroom, then my window of opportunity is gone. It is therefore important to me that I use the time that I have identified when it is available to me.

Freedom: It may seem strange to suggest that freedom is the third necessary ingredient, but I have discovered that it is most important. By freedom I understand a certain "stance toward life," a "permission to be myself and to be gentle and understanding of who I am." I am constantly amazed at how the human person so easily sets himself or herself up for disappointment and perceived failure. We so easily make judgments about ourselves and our actions and our choices, and very often those judgments are negative, and not at all helpful.

For instance, what does it really matter if I have chosen a place and a time, and I have missed both the place and the time for three days in a row? What does it matter if I have chosen, in that twilight time before I am completely awake and still a little sleepy, to roll over and to sleep for fifteen minutes more? Does it mean that I am not serious about the journey, that I really don't want to pray, that I am just fooling myself when I say that my prayer time is important to me? Perhaps, but I prefer to believe that it simply means that I am tired and I just wanted a little more sleep. It doesn't mean anything more than that. However, if I make it mean more than that, then I can become discouraged, frustrated, and put myself into a state where I might more easily give up. "What's the use? I might as well forget all about it."

The same sense of freedom applies to the reading and the praying of this text. If I do not find the introduction to each day helpful, I don't need to read it. If I find the questions for reflection at the end of the appointed day repetitive, then I should choose to close the book and go my own way. Even if I discover that the reflection offered for the day is not the one that I prefer and that the one for the next day seems more inviting, then by all means, go on to the one for the next day.

That's it! If you apply these simple rules to your journey you should receive the maximum benefit and you will soon find yourself at your destination. But be prepared to be surprised. If you have never been on a spiritual journey you should know that the "travel brochures" and the other descriptions that you might have heard are nothing compared to the real thing. There is so much more than you can imagine.

A final prayer of blessing suggests itself:

> Lord, catch me off guard today.
> Surprise me with some moment of beauty
>   or pain
> So that at least for the moment
> I may be startled into seeing that you are
>   here in all your splendor,
> Always and everywhere,
> Barely hidden,
> Beneath,
> Beyond,
> Within this life I breathe.

Frederick Buechner

REV. THOMAS M. SANTA, CSsR
LIGUORI, MISSOURI
FEAST OF THE PRESENTATION, 1999

A Brief Chronology of Saint Dominic's Life

SAINT DOMINIC WAS A MAN who took his strength and wisdom from his intense prayer life. It is said of him that he was either speaking to or about God. He taught the friars of his order (the Order of Friars Preachers or the Dominicans) that their preaching must begin with quiet prayer and studying. One of their mottos is "Give to others the fruits of your contemplation." The spirits of contemplation, preaching, humility, poverty, and service are the foundation stones of the order and its members.

Dominic's character was said to be one of extraordinary integrity and sensitivity. He was a disciplined student, both scholastically and spiritually. His order has stood for the value of all things divine as well as those of temporal mankind, welcoming new ideas, while remaining faithful to those "tried and true" principles of the past. Saint Dominic said: "A man who governs his passions is the master of his world. We must either command them or be enslaved by them. It is better to be a hammer than an anvil."

1170–1204:

Dominic is born (in 1170) in Calaruega, Castile (Spain), to Felix Guzman and Blessed Joan of Aza, the youngest of four children; his father was the town warden; their family was of the nobility.

His first education came from his uncle, the archpriest of Gumiel, then, for ten years, at the University of Palencia (he entered at the age of fourteen); he graduated with a degree in liberal arts and sacred sciences.

Ordained at the age of twenty-four, he was invited by Bishop Diego of Osma to join his reformed canons regular.

1205–1214:

Dominic accompanied Diego on various missions across Europe; upon their return, they stopped to see Pope Innocent III to ask to be released from their duties in order to be able to go on foreign missions. The pope had been looking for men to go and fight heresy in southern France (especially against the Albigensians) at that time. It was an era of transition and unrest in society in general. Many groups had "sprouted" up calling themselves religious, but teaching heretical practices. Feeling that their needs were greater at home, the pope sent Diego and Dominic to southern France. The Cistercians assisted by sending monks to help them.

By April 1207, there were forty missionaries, but they were having little lasting success. A disaster befell them by year's end: the Cistercians returned home discouraged; Diego died while on his trip home to garner replacements; one legate was assassinated by heretics.

At one point, Dominic became discouraged at the lack of progress of the mission. In 1208, he reported receiving a vision from Our Lady in the Church of Prouille, who showed him a wreath of roses, telling him to say the rosary daily and to teach it to all who would listen. (Dominic is often credited with the invention of the rosary; some historical sources say that it predates him, yet thirteen popes support the claim that he did invent it.)

Dominic remained in Prouille for six years (some sources say four, others eight), in spite of a civil war; during this time he founded a religious community of women. These women were converts from heresy and his only helpers.

1215–1220:

Peace came (in 1215) and Dominic was asked to assist in a general reform and reorganization by the bishop of Toulouse. By the end of the year, Dominic proposed to Pope Innocent that they should found a worldwide order of preachers—consent was given.

Dominic was asked to create a constitution and, one year later, the Order of Friars Preachers (also known as the Dominicans) was approved (under a new pope—Honorius III).

Dominic now had sixteen followers; they were sent to be educated and then to serve all over Europe; he, himself, traveled on foot throughout Europe organizing the order.

In 1218, he began the Confraternity of the Rosary.

In 1220, Dominic convened the first Chapter at Bologna; the final constitution of the order was determined: historians have called it one of the most remarkable legislative achievements in western Christianity.

Dominicans were sent to England, Hungary, Denmark, and Greece; Dominic spent the final years of his life traveling to Italy, Spain, and France to preach, attract new members, and establish new houses.

1221: Dominic died at Bologna on August 6 (some sources report it as August 4), after illness forced him to return from a tour of Hungary.

Dominic was canonized by Pope Gregory IX on July 13, 1234 (just thirteen years after his death). His feast day is August 8.

The new Dominican order was remarkably successful in conversion since it applied Dominic's concept of harmonizing the intellectual life with the needs of the people. Dominic is known as the patron saint of astronomers.

Introduction

PRAY WITH SAINT DOMINIC

We could not find a better master of the spiritual life than Saint Dominic. But we must not be anachronistic. It would be vain to seek a doctrine from him like we would find with John of the Cross, Teresa of Ávila, or Ignatius of Loyola. They belong to a century of "spiritualities," and from the Holy Spirit they received the grace to give, to those souls which are in search of communion, points of reference for their progress. That is how an individual's spiritual life is structured. When accompanied by a good guide, each of us can see where he or she is and make progress.

This is not the case with Saint Dominic. His concerns were not his own. To ask that service of him would be to mistake the era in which he lived. Above all, Saint Dominic leaves us an example. Those who see a model for their Christian life in him and feel that they are called to live as he did, must make the effort to reinvent and adapt their own situation according to the three inseparable axes of Dominic's life: apostolic zeal, community life, and intensive prayer.

Above all, in fact, Dominic was a man who never missed an occasion to proclaim the gospel. All of those who were witnesses attested to that. The following is a particularly good example:

Brother Dominic was full of pity for his neighbors and very ardently desired their salvation. He preached frequently and, by all of the means within his power, urged the brothers to preach and sent them out to do so; he then warned and beseeched them to be full of concern for the salvation of souls (VIE, disposition of Jean d'Espagne, no. 26).

Community life is one characteristic of his foundation. The Order of Saint Dominic does not rest solely on the auspices of one man, like the abbatial formula of the Rule of Saint Benedict does, but on the community of brothers, on the concertation, the fraternal consensus, the communal remittance of everyone's goods, the communal celebration of the liturgy, the election of superiors at all levels, and so on. Saint Dominic, who gave it great importance, had the genius to put into practice a durable organization in his order that united the free expression of the personalities of the brothers and continuous change, as much for their laws as for their ordinary, everyday lives.

Another memory we have of Saint Dominic is of a man of prayer. Dominic prayed everywhere and constantly. He who walked so much, prayed on the roads so that he wouldn't lose contact with the Lord. If he heard the bells of a monastery, he would go and join the monks and sing the Liturgy of the Hours with them. He made pilgrimages to Rocamadour and Rome. But, above all, he prayed in the convent in the midst of his brothers. Witnesses to his almost daily Masses noted that he was moved to the point of tears at the thought of the passion of the Savior. He wanted his brothers to be present and fervent, and he never missed reminding them of this vigorously. But the aspect that was the most remarkable to his brothers were his nights of prayer, with his wailing that could be heard throughout the corridors. He prayed with his body, standing up, bending over, and laying, face-down, on the ground.

> It was, in fact, a meeting that barely interrupted with his Master, the crucified Christ, whom he met through the books of the New Testament which he carried with him. He knew them practically by heart. In the middle of the Church, along with the apostles, he and his brothers gave adoration, praise, and thanksgiving to the Father. But, above all, they interceded. That was the principal theme of Saint Dominic's prayers. Even when he prayed alone in his endless vigils, he did not separate himself from others. His dialogue with Christ always had the same theme—the souls for whom Christ had given his life (EVA, p. 14).

That is the man of God who we will be following for the next fifteen days. May the Lord grant us the grace to be like him.

Abbreviations Used in This Book

The majority of the texts cited are taken from documents which have been edited by Father M. H. Vicaire, O.P. They have appeared in two volumes:

—*Saint Dominic, The Apostolic Life (Saint Dominique, La vie apostolique)*, Paris, Cerf, 1953 (reference edition 1965);

—*Saint Dominic and His Brothers, Gospel or Crusade (Saint Dominique et ses frères, Évangile ou croisade)*, Paris, Cerf, 1967.

(English translation of titles added)

VIE   *Saint Dominic, The Apostolic Life*

EVA   *Saint Dominic and His Brothers...*

LIB   *Libellus* (edited in c. 1233–1234 by Jourdain of Saxe, Dominic's successor as head of the Order of the Friars Preachers, published in *Saint Dominic and His Brothers...*)

M   *Saint Dominic's Nine Ways of Prayer* (used as follows: M1 is the first way; M2 is the second way, and so on), published in *Saint Dominic, The Apostolic Life*

15 Days of Prayer
With Saint Dominic

DAY ONE

A Man of Compassion

FOCUS POINT

Dominic abhorred poverty, yet sought it out. Material poverty, the misery of the less fortunate, moved him to great compassion, to give up his material attachments and unite his soul with that of the one who was suffering. Dominic sought out the spiritual poverty that allows a person to be free of attachments, and open to another. This is our goal, as well. How close to God will we be when we seek the poverty of spirit that invites God—makes room for only him—into our lives.

A great famine spread across practically all of Spain when Dominic was studying in Palencia. Moved by the distress of the poor, and burning with compassion inside, he resolved through a single action to both obey the words of the Lord as

*well as ease the misery of the dying poor as best he could. He
then sold all of the books he owned (no matter how indispensable) and all of his possessions. By turning these into alms, he
distributed his goods and gave them to the poor (LIB, no. 10).*

The compassion that touched the heart of the young student who had contact with the misery of the poor never
left him. Mercy is the first trait that is characteristic of Saint
Dominic's personality. In order to begin this fifteen-day retreat with him, we must determine what compassion dwells in
our hearts.

Just as the word says, "compassion" is this interior attrib-
ute which puts us in communion with the misery of another
person. The Lord Jesus had this compassion. He suffered with
those who suffered. He shared their pain. He transmitted this
sensitivity to his disciples. Man's misery moved him.

The young Dominic resembled the rich young man (in the
Bible) who would have followed through to the end. Like him,
he went to the Lord. He wanted to obtain eternal life. He already practiced the commandments. And when, interiorly, he
heard the order to sell all of his goods, he did it spontaneously,
for he felt it was pressing. He did not give what he had that
was extraneous. He gave what was most useful to him, what
he needed the most—his books, those which were annotated
personally by him.

The Lord Jesus, sensitive to the hunger of the crowd, mul-
tiplied the bread and fish. Dominic did what a man could do,
but which few men do. He gave what he had. He didn't talk
about poverty, he did what was most pressing, what his heart
told him to do. Just like Saint Vincent de Paul would later do,

he did not seek to resolve all the problems of hunger in the world. He did what he could. But he had the courage to do what he could do.

Brother Étienne, one of his first friars and one of the few in his confidence, gave the following testimony at the cause for his canonization:

> Completely moved with compassion and mercy, Brother Dominic sold his personally annotated books and gave the proceeds to the poor, as well as other things he owned. He said: "I don't want to use these dead skins (books) to study when there are men who are dying of hunger" (VIE, no, 35).

Dominic was not sentimental, he was a man of compassion. He was particularly sensitive. He could not stand to see man live in misery. If he reacted, at a young age, to the material poverty caused by famine, later, he reacted to the moral poverty of those who fell into heresy.

Dominic was a man of compassion. With his friend and contemporary, Brother Francis of Assisi, he shared this need to imitate Christ in his poverty. He perceived that Christ's true poverty was not material, not a concern about where he laid his head. He manifested his true poverty by not using rank as a requirement for access to God. It was also manifested in the compassion that he felt seeing the sheep without a shepherd.

From the Holy Spirit, Dominic received this gift of sharing the suffering of others. His own vocation was triggered by this compassion. When he discovered the poverty of those who had turned away from the true faith and the Church through Catharistic heretical preachers who had found refuge in southwestern France after having been chased away from everywhere else, he was upset by it. Ways of thinking have changed over the centuries; we do not know Dominic as a critic of the heretics. It would be more correct to see him as a man of extreme sensitivity. Properly said, he could not "stand the sight" of these people!

There are numerous witnesses who saw him in tears. Like Jesus cried about Jerusalem's indifference to his message of love, Dominic cried about the misery of the poor. He also cried when he celebrated Mass, when he made Christ's passion become his own. He suffered with him that God is not loved as he should be. He suffered with him that man didn't receive the message of the gospel which speaks only of God's love for man.

This compassion did not remain just theoretical; it would change Dominic's life. He would let himself be guided by it. It was compassion that would change the course of his life. And if he decided to remain in Lauragais instead of going home to continue his well-regimented life, it was because he perceived a call with such a force that he couldn't resist it.

Dominic was a man of compassion. Later, we would see that he wasn't a frail person, someone who would whine or go weak at the knees when things got difficult, when blood would flow. He was completely capable of making his own decisions. But at the very depth of himself, it was his heart that spoke.

More than once, he would be his brothers' consoler. If he saw a brother having a problem, he would dedicate himself to him. He would speak to him, urging him to trust in divine Providence. His words were so gentle, they said, and he so well perceived the pain in that brother's life, that the brother would leave consoled and comforted.

That was a characteristic of the blessed Dominic, one which

Sister Cecile, one of the first religious of his order, often heard in the parlor of her monastery, where he had lived for a number of years: "He was always smiling and happy, unless he was moved with compassion by some affliction of his neighbor" (VIE, p. 124).

We could say that Saint Dominic had the sensitivity of a woman, that intuition which works without words ever being spoken, that delicate attention that knows what comforting action to take at the appropriate moment.

His successor as head of the order also gives us a portrait of him in his *Libellus*, a booklet that he wrote for "the brothers who wanted to know the circumstances of the foundation and the beginning of the Order of Friars Preachers" (LIB, no. 2). This is what he said:

> In him, he had a very firm equality of soul except when some troubling concern excited his compassion and mercy (LIB, no. 103).

Further on, this other remark, which in a few words addressed a touching scene and gave us a spiritual portrait:

> He welcomed all people into the vast embrace of his charity and, since he loved the entire world, everyone loved him. He made it his own personal rule to be happy with those people who were happy and to cry with those who were sad, overflowing with religious affection and devoting himself completely to taking care of his neighbor and sympathizing with people in misery (LIB, no. 107).

Dominic lived this compassion for another's misery very spontaneously. Having been completely filled with the Lord Jesus and letting him live within him, he acquired his reflexes. He couldn't pass a poor person without being affected. He had this heart of flesh that creates true men of God, true theologians, like one of the sons of his order, Saint Thomas Aquinas, would later say.

As well, Saint Dominic had wanted his brothers to participate in this same compassion. He wanted them to go to preach, prompted by this sole urge: to give to mankind, in their moral, material, and spiritual poverty, the response that flows from God's heart. And so that they stay sensitive, so that their hearts don't become hardened to it, and not forget their reason for being, he asked them to love poverty.

For him, poverty was the sign by which one recognized preachers who were truly available to God, preachers who truly loved Christ to the point of giving themselves completely to him to do what he would with them. Numerous testimonials about him say that he was a "true lover of poverty" (LIB, no. 108).

On the first day of this retreat with Saint Dominic, we will meditate with him upon this immense love that burned in the heart of our Lord Jesus Christ, this love that led him all the way to the cross, this love that is spread to the hearts of the faithful.

REFLECTION QUESTIONS

Am I moved by the material poverty I witness in the lives of others? How do I respond to this? Do I take an active role in helping to relieve this suffering? In what ways do I unite myself in compassion with the one who is suffering? Do I seek to reach these people on a face-to-face level? Do I seek out the poverty of spirit and freedom from attachments that allow this unity between myself and God, myself and others, to flourish?

A Man of Decision

FOCUS POINT

To know what is right and to act upon it: both halves of this statement are so very important. To have the knowledge of what is right is not enough in itself. One must also have the courage to act upon that knowledge. If we are not living the gospel we hear at Mass, that we read in our Bible, then we are not truly living in God. We are hearing but not listening. God graces us with so much. Let us be open to prudence and fortitude so that, like Saint Dominic, we will know the right course of action and possess the courage and determination to see it through.

*He (Brother Dominic) invoked the Holy Spirit, and convened
all of his brothers and told them that he had, in his heart,
made a decision to send them all over the world in spite of
their small number and, from that time on, they would no
longer live together in that place. Each one was astonished to
hear him proclaim such a categorical decision so quickly taken.
But the manifest authority that holiness gave him engulfed them
so much that they agreed easily, full of hope with respect to
the happy result of this decision (LIB, no. 47).*

But all would be fulfilled through a divine instinct.

*It was astonishing to see how the servant of God, Master
Dominic, when he sent brothers here and there, into the various areas of the Church of God, as we have already seen, did
it with certainty, without hesitation, nor wavering, even though
others, at the same time, thought that it should not be done.
Everything happened as if the future was a certainty, or as if
the Holy Spirit had taught him through his revelations (LIB,
no. 62).*

D ominic's compassion never prevented him from making a
decision. To the contrary, the important decisions that
marked his life were a result of his compassion. He felt interiorly pushed to take the routes that he had not seen before. The
same urgency spurred him on. It was an urgency to feed those
who were hungry, as well as an urgency to deviate from the
way that had been already planned.

The first major decision was the one to remain in
Languedoc. At that time, he still depended upon his bishop,
Diego of Osma. It was he who, upon returning from Curie,
stayed with the legates the pope had sent to meet the Cathars.

They stayed for two years. Then Diego decided to return to his diocese, which he had neglected for too long a time. In his place, he left his subprior, Brother Dominic. He left him to continue his mission.

> He gave spiritual control of those who remained to Brother Dominic, because he was truly filled with the Holy Spirit of God (LIB, no. 29).

Not only did Brother Dominic not make the least objection, he definitively remained in this country which was not his own, but which he adopted through his love for God. He began by staying at Fanjeaux for nine years.

Here, we can admire Brother Dominic's docility. He made the bishop's intuition become his own before undertaking it and gave it a greater amplitude. For the spirit of decision goes in concert with docility. A person who knows how to give orders is someone who first knows how to obey, not to obey through a lack of ideas of one's own or through a weakness of character; but to obey by voluntarily agreeing to a superior proposition. Dominic had been an incomparable leader because he knew how to enter into a project that was not, at the onset, solely his own idea.

The decision having been made, Dominic would not go back on it. He had given up everything in order to dedicate himself to his new task. The spirit of decision means nothing unless it is accompanied by perseverance. Dominic manifested as much tenacity as decisiveness. He knew how to endure whatever he undertook. That is what his contemporaries called "his very firm equality of soul" (LIB, no. 103). When he agreed to remain in France, as well as when he sent his brothers to the four corners of Europe, as much for the very important occasions as well as in the details of ordinary life, Dominic didn't equivocate. It seems as if he was pushed by the brevity of his life (in fact, he would die at the age of fifty-one) and the urgency of his mission.

We must believe that this characteristic of his spiritual attitude was not common since those close to him noted:

> He kept such a constancy in affairs that he judged reasonable before God to maintain, that he never, or nearly never, agreed to modify a decision that had been taken after much deliberation (LIB, no. 103).

It is an understatement to say that it must not have been easy to live on a daily basis with someone with such tremendous drive. We know that he prayed at length before making a decision. We venerate his holiness. But we also know that once the decision was made, it was practically useless to try to get it changed.

What is considered stubbornness with normal persons appears to be a virtue for saints! And yet Dominic knew how to bend to the will of his brothers. He, a man of decision, wanted to give his brothers the chance to decide as well. Not for each to decide for himself, which would cause many problems and disorder, but to decide together—that would be more difficult. Dominic gave his brothers the chance to make decisions on more than one occasion.

First, they had the choice of the rule with which they would use to found this new order. And that was only their initial choice. This is what the *Libellus* tells us about Brother Dominic's stay in Rome for the Fourth Lateran Council:

When the presentation of their request had been heard,
the Bishop of Rome invited Brother Dominic to return
to his brothers to deliberate with them about this, then,
with their unanimous consent, to swear and to profess
their allegiance to whatever rule that they had agreed
upon.

Thus, after the celebration of the council, they returned and relayed the reply of the pope. Soon after,
these future friars preachers made their profession to
the Rule of Saint Augustine, the eminent preacher (LIB,
no. 41–42).

We should note the key words "deliberate with" and "unanimous consent." That is the entire essence of Dominic. He was
not only a man of decision, he also knew how to bring about a
decision: "Brother Dominic was so good that he brought the
brothers of his order to abandon and scorn all temporal goods,
and so on…" (VIE, p. 53). He was gentle, yet firm.

It did happen that, on occasion, he would bend when faced
with a decision by the brothers that was different from his
own. And that was not with respect to a minor matter. It was
with reference to the statute about the lay (those religious who
are not ordained) brothers, those religious who participated in
the communal vocation of the order for the salvation of souls,
not by preaching, but through service and menial tasks in the
convents. Brother Dominic wanted to give them full power in
this area.

So that the brothers apply themselves with more energy to study and preaching, Brother Dominic wanted
the illiterate lay brothers of his order to govern over
those who were educated in those things which ap-

plied to the administration and maintenance of temporal things. But the clerical brothers did not want to let themselves be dominated by the lay brothers (VIE, p. 53, deposition of Brother Jean d'Espagne during the process for canonization in Bologna).

For Dominic, the true spiritual gift was the art of making a good decision, along with knowing when to accept the decision of the community. That doesn't happen because of a certain temperament or a change of attitude. He possessed, in an eminent way, the cardinal virtue of prudence. What had to be done was thought out deeply within him. He questioned the Lord through intense prayer. Once he decided, he didn't waver.

For those who want to learn from Saint Dominic, there is a lesson here not to be overlooked or neglected. There would be, in fact, a real danger in allowing oneself to be touched by misery, if it were to stop there. Our emotions are not good counselors if they are not accompanied by the will to act. And we must also know what to do. It is useless to dream of impossible objectives. It is useless to throw oneself into directions that have not been first evaluated. On the other hand, it would be disheartening to become discouraged even before undertaking something and decide to do nothing.

Saint Dominic gives us an example of someone with a true spirit of decision. Gifted with a fertile imagination, he was filled with boldness when it concerned serving God and the gospel. He was as realistic as he was docile, and he allowed himself to be guided by the Holy Spirit. The gift of counsel brought the best fruit to him.

His brothers and sisters loved this characteristic of his spiritual portrait. From then on, it became a part of the *Domini-*

can spirit which tries to put this old adage into action: "That which has to be lived by everyone, must be decided upon by everyone," to which must be added an indispensable phrase: "that which has been decided upon for everyone, must be lived by each!"

REFLECTION QUESTIONS

How often in my life have I known the right thing to do (or not to do) only to give into fear or temptation? Do I pray for God's grace at these times of weakness? It is easier to do what is less demanding in times that call for determination and perseverance. Do I recognize the unity, peace, and joy that come with persevering through struggle, and adhering to what I know is right and good? Does the life I lead mirror the gospel I profess as my guide? When I do fail, am I willing to forgive myself and be forgiven by God so that I might carry on?

DAY THREE

A Man of Conviction

FOCUS POINT

When Dominic went about forming his order of preachers according to the gospel model of Jesus and his apostles, Dominic understood that nothing must prevent the preaching model of the gospel from being fully realized. Brothers must be able to live in community as the apostles did, with a strict adherence to a life of poverty. Dominic stood by this conviction: there would be no revenue taken in by his order. Their mission was one—to preach the gospel of Jesus Christ without impediment.

I was not amongst the very first brothers, but I lived with them; I saw and was quite familiar with the blessed Dominic himself, not only outside of the order, but in the order after I entered; I took the habit only four years after the institution of the order. It seemed a good idea for me to write down all of the events that happened in the order: those which I personally saw and heard, or those I knew about through a relationship with the founding brothers; those about the beginning of the order; about the life and miracles of our blessed Father Dominic.... Thus, our brothers yet to be born will grow up knowing about the beginnings of the order and will have their questions answered. For time goes by so quickly that there will soon be no one left who would be able to tell the true story about its origins (LIB, no. 3).

The brothers and sisters of the order recognized the Blessed Jourdain of Saxe as having the prudence to record the beginnings of the Dominican order. For this constituted the inauguration of a reality that was very new in the Church.

In fact, Saint Dominic inaugurated a new way to live the religious life of the era. He installed "the apostolic life," that is, a life that followed the example given by the apostles. He didn't only receive a personal religious vocation from heaven; he received that of being a founder of an order, a vocation that is reserved for very few. At the beginning, Dominic had received the vocation of a regular "canon": one who belonged to a diocese; he was a part of the bishop's clerics. Then he was called to be the head of a completely new reality through which institutions would be invented. To be truthful, the idea had been in the air at the time. Many had made the attempt to create this new form of religious life. It needed someone who could put it into place and solidly organize it.

Dominic received this privilege. He would endow the Church with a body of brothers who were organized for "the apostolic life." Then the Church organized the religious life into *orders*, just like it would later organize itself into *congregations*. We are all acquainted with many religious orders. Saint Francis founded an *order* whose vocation was to preach about Christ the poor person as a poor person, Dominic founded an *order* of preachers to imitate Christ the preacher of the gospel.

To illustrate this, there was an anecdote that ran through the Order of Saint Dominic early on. It was passed from one generation to the next, each person finding an illustration of what he wanted to live:

At the time when the Apostle (that is, the pope) came to confirm the order, he asked the notary to put the name of the preaching brothers into the address. Or, by finalizing the letter of confirmation, writing it directly as: brothers preachers. Having re-read the letter, the pope said to the notary: why didn't you put preaching brothers like I said to you, and why have you decided to write brothers preachers? Without getting upset, he replied: preaching is an adjective, we can concede that the participle could substantiate it and make it a common noun in act; but preacher is properly a substantive, and, at the same time, a verbal as well as personal noun which declares and manifests both the name and the function. Dear readers, see with what justice the notary refuted the objections? Preaching would never signify its contents other than through the mode of a passing action; but preacher signifies it through a mode of possession, even if it isn't always an action. It was very suitable to put preachers, and the Lord Apostle, having surrendered to these evident reasons, granted the order the name preacher in its title, which was solemnly confirmed by the cardinals (EVA, p. 87).

This story is as plausible as not; the bull of confirmation, kept in the archives at Carcassonne, shows some traces of the change. And this change is significant. Dominic, in effect, didn't ask for authorization, for either his brothers or himself, to preach temporarily in Toulouse or in any other region. He had a vision that was much bolder, nothing less than instituting a way of life that closely copied what the apostles lived in Jerusalem after the Pentecost.

This *apostolic life* brought two inseparable elements with it: the communal life and the proclamation of the gospel. Today, let us meditate on the communal life to which Dominic attached such importance.

Communal life should not be presented as a juxtaposition of individuals living in a team. It takes the whole individual, body and soul. Materially, it implies the indispensable action of communally pooling all goods. In effect, when the members of a community possess nothing of their own, they are truly dependent upon each other. That creates a mentality that could be nothing other than a fraternal one; if not, it will mean death just as it did in the story of Ananias and Sapphira (see Acts 5:1ff).

Communal life equally implies community prayer. The apostle's prayer is the prayer of the Church: the divine liturgy that tirelessly celebrates the Resurrection of the Lord. We will come back to this later in this book.

Communal life, if it is to be harmonious and a harbor of peace, implies even more that we truly live under the same roof and in a state of unanimity. Unanimity is the transcription into our daily lives of: "Now the whole group of those who believed were of one heart and soul…" (Acts 4:32). Saint Dominic had been particularly concerned about this. He knew that the brothers would only remain together if they had an interest in being of one mind. If Saint Benedict's adage had been *habitare secum* (live with yourself), that of Saint Dominic would be *convivere conventualiter* (live together in community).

Poverty was also a part of this communal life. Dominic, by opting for this way of life, asked that his brothers deprive themselves of the revenue which the religious of the time normally received. Right at the beginning, Dominic had accepted a few properties, it was the time when "The Order of Preachers had not yet been instituted. We had only treated it as an institution, even though Brother Dominic had put all of his energies into the ministry of preaching" (LIB, no. 37). But quickly, Dominic became aware that, for more than one reason, they must not have any revenue: the freedom of preaching, availability of the brothers, imitation of Jesus, and so on, pushed him to be strict in this aspect.

Not only did Dominic "like poverty and urge his brothers to practice it" (VIE, p. 58), he came to the point of categorically refusing to accept anything that was susceptible to become a source of revenue. The reason behind this was that he wanted his brothers to be solely occupied with preaching, to which he added study and prayer. He made them become mendicants (friars), under which label they are known. This mendicancy took on various forms according to the times. Today, as always, it consists of having no revenue and living on what Providence would give to the brothers. Whatever may be received is shared by the community.

Dominic, a man of conviction, did not waver. He knew

that the vitality of the apostolic life depended upon it. Even in death, he urged his brothers to practice voluntary poverty.

Those who want to learn from Saint Dominic will meditate upon this requirement.

REFLECTION QUESTIONS

How do the convictions I hold in my own life affect my relationship with God? What attachments serve as obstacles to my living the gospel of Jesus Christ to the fullest? How do I deal with these obstacles? Am I even aware of their presence in my life? Might I pray for greater awareness of whatever obstacle may be keeping me from serving God to the fullest in my life? When I recognize the obstacles in my life, do I see them for what they truly are—less than God, an obstacle to happiness—and leave them behind so that I might grow in service to Jesus Christ?

DAY FOUR

A Man of God

FOCUS POINT

Dominic's life was devoted fully to God. It was said that when he spoke, Dominic was either speaking to God in prayer or speaking of God to his listener. A life in God brought Dominic great joy, and Dominic gave everything that he was in service to God. There is great joy in God because there is freedom in God: freedom from worry, fear, and sin. God is our Lord and provider of all that is good and joyful. Like Dominic, let us live our lives for God and God alone.

The holy father also saw God through contemplation. The blessed father often voluntarily visited the places of prayer and the corporal relics of the saints. He did not hold back: he frequently prayed day and night. Often, each time he had the

chance, he went to a city named Castres, in the diocese of Albi,
which was next to that of Toulouse, in order to pray to and
honor the Blessed Vincent, deacon, whose body we know, with
certainty, lies in that Church (EVA, p. 82).

W ithout question, Brother Dominic loved the Lord. The
chronicler above shows him going on pilgrimage, that
was just one example of his profound attachment to the Lord.

Dominic appears to be a man of profound faith. From a
young age, he seems to have had an intimate relationship with
Christ. Very early on, he dedicated his life to him, not only by
consecrating himself to the priesthood, but also by manifesting a piety that startled his contemporaries. Everyone was astonished by it and spoke of it. Testimonies that were gathered
with a view to his canonization abound in this aspect, and we
must remember that he was canonized a mere thirteen years
after his death. Many of those who spoke at that time knew
him personally.

For example, Father Guillaume of Montferrat declared that:

Brother Dominic gave him the impression of a very
religious man, more religious than he had met to date
(...); he seemed to him to have more zeal for the salvation of man than anyone else he had ever known (VIE,
p. 43).

It is so true that, for him, the love of God and the love for
one's neighbor are connected.

Here is the very moving testimony of Brother Paul of Venice,
another of his companions. He declared that:

When they traveled together, he saw him pray, preach, and give himself to the meditation of God. Master Dominic said to him: "Go on ahead and let us think of our Savior." No matter where they were, he continuously either spoke about God or with God (VIE, p. 68).

We are struck by "the spark of divine fervor that carried him" (LIB, no. 103). It was this intense interior life that shows in this portrait that all are making for us of this man who spent the majority of his time either speaking to God, or speaking about God to someone.

This theological life expressed itself in happiness, this fruit of true charity. Dominic left behind the mark of a man who was filled with joy. He who had made us so tangibly see the misery of others let the Lord dwell within him to the point of no longer being affected by whatever happened to him. Brother Paul of Venice "never saw Master Dominic show anger, emotion, or be troubled, neither following a trip, nor in the fire of passion, nor in any circumstance; rather, he saw him happy through trials and patient in adversity" (VIE, p. 68).

This gift of happiness, which comes from God, bequethed a particular fortune after the death of the founder of this order. All of the witnesses reported that, at the time when his remains were being transferred from their temporary resting place (where he was placed just after he died) to the tomb they built for him at the convent of Bologna, a strange thing happened.

"They feared that Dominic's body, which had, for a time, been subjected to rain and the temperature, hidden in a makeshift tomb, would be crawling with maggots and smell bad" (LIB, no. 127), but just the opposite happened! From the tomb came an odor that no one had ever smelled. It was not just one or two brothers who testified to this, but all who had been present, and there were quite a few. The Blessed Jourdain, Dominic's successor, attested that his hands emitted this perfume (LIB, no. 128). Brother Rudolph, who had buried Dominic in his first tomb, certified that no perfume had been deposited there. And it was he, who "with iron chains demolished the wall of the tomb which had been very resistant and was built with strong and hard cement. It was he who lifted the upper slab with an iron bar. (...) And at the moment when he lifted this stone with the iron bar, a strong odor, a very strong odor, that was sweet and delectable, which he didn't recognize, escaped from there" (VIE, p. 60).

Perhaps our rational senses don't really believe in, or attach any great value to this good odor, the holy odor. Perhaps we don't know how to be sensitive or open to this type of manifestation of holiness? When we read other texts of that era, we can easily see that people's feelings have not changed at all. The brothers were in no hurry to see the tomb of their father opened. They feared the bad odors and all the other possible ideas attached to opening it. Their unanimity in attesting to what happened proves their astonishment. But it appeared to be a sign for them from heaven. The happiness that Dominic had while he lived on earth continues now through this odor. It spreads in perfusion and gives happiness to all who are its beneficiaries. The good odor and happiness are connected, just like bad odor and sadness are.

This perfume that came from Saint Dominic's remains appears to us to be a confirmation, from heaven, of his theological life. He lived in faith and hope. He lived perfect charity with respect to God and his neighbor. He knew happiness, even in the midst of trials. He was radiant and shone with this divine life that dwelled within. He continued to shine with happiness after his death.

On this fourth day of our retreat, we breathe in this lovely perfumed example which Saint Dominic leaves for us. We ask the Lord to give us the same radiance which proceeds from a profound communion with him.

REFLECTION QUESTIONS

How do I respond to the fact that when Saint Dominic spoke it was either to God or about God? Do I treasure my words in the same way? How do I use words throughout my day? Are they rooted in God or do they result from fear, hate, or sin? Perhaps I can try to be more aware of the way in which I use words in my daily life. If I make my life more God-centered (and my words are a part of that), the abiding joy that Dominic knew will be a constant in my own life.

DAY FIVE

A Man of Prayer

FOCUS POINT

Dominic was a man of prayer, both formally and informally. His nights were given to God in deep prayer; Dominic stood in prayer, his arms extended as if he were on a cross. During the day, and more informally than in the evening, Dominic lived his prayer in service to others, always keeping in mind the great importance of the salvation of souls. Like Dominic, our prayer lives must extend beyond formality and into the practice of life situations. In doing this, we incorporate the gospel into our life's work and leisure so that our whole life is prayer.

The blessed Dominic never went to bed before praying for a prolonged period, often with such moaning, sighs, and noise so loud that he awakened his companions.... He passed more time praying than sleeping. (...) He abstained from idle chatter and spoke either with God or about him (VIE, p. 44).

———

All of those who knew Dominic, either from near or far, as close friends or just acquaintances, attested to the intensity of his prayers. Dominic prayed like he breathed. He was not one of those who had time to write books, not even books on prayer, he just prayed. He spent the majority of his time in prayer. He entered into a state of prayer as naturally and rapidly as others fell asleep. To spontaneously fall asleep is a childhood grace. Dominic was a child according to the gospel, a child who dove into prayer whenever he had a moment, most especially during the night. For him, the night was made for prayer.

Even when he was just a young religious, he already appeared to be a man specially gifted for prayer:

> Night and day, like the olive tree that produces fruit or the cypress that reaches to the heavens, he used the floor of the church, devoting his time to contemplation, never appearing to leave the monastery. God had given him the special grace of prayer for sinners, the poor, the afflicted: he carried their maladies in the intimate sanctuary of his compassion; and the tears that came boiling from his eyes manifested the ardor of the feelings that burned within him. It was his habit to spend his nights in prayer. With the door closed, he prayed to his

Father. During and at the end of his prayers, he uttered moans which came from his heart. He couldn't hold back, and these cries, coming spontaneously, could clearly be heard up above in heaven (LIB, no. 12).

Dominic, like a beacon of light that burns in the night, realized the Lord's precept: "Be alert at all times, praying..." (Lk 21:36). He didn't just make the motions when he prayed; all of his being became a prayer, he prayed with both body and soul. He became inflamed for the Lord. He burned with love for him. For him, there was an urgency in prayer. He had no time to lose. Souls were what would be lost, there was the threat to lose those who had problems. He had to intervene immediately.

Saint Dominic prayed with his entire being. He didn't only pray with his head or with his heart, he prayed with his entire body. His prayer was not only a mental one, but it was one of gestures.

It was the same for the abundant tears that flowed from his eyes. They visibly expressed his profound communion with the passion of those who were suffering. These weren't just occasional tears, brought on by something that moved him for the moment. He was always in tears, for he continuously had the passion of his Lord and his contemporaries in his sight.

When studying with Saint Dominic, we learn to pray with our entire being. In order to imitate him, one must first observe him, just as Sister Cecile did; she never tired of watching her Master pray. The contents of his prayer were expressed by his behaviors.

In order to truly be present to the "true presence" of the One whom we are addressing, we must first prostrate ourselves with faith before him. Thus, at times Dominic prayed

"humbly, prostrate before the altar, as if Jesus Christ, represented by this altar, was truly and personally present" (M1).

In order to express the attitude of humility, the only one
that suits the person who is conscious of his worthlessness, he
must do it with *humus* (humility) and profoundly prostrate his
body as well as his being (attitude). "The blessed Dominic often prayed completely stretched out, face-down on the ground"
(M2).

Just as the Christian's prayer is, above all, an imitation of
Christ as he prays, and Jesus Christ's prayer reached its perfection on the cross, the Christian knows that he must pass through
the cross in true prayer. To contemplate the cross, embrace it,
to lash oneself to it (as Fra Angelico often depicted Saint
Dominic in his paintings) is to prolong the sacrifice of the Mass,
and enter into Jesus' own prayer. Thus, Saint Dominic particularly liked to contemplate the crucifix. "He considered it with
an incomparable penetration. Before it, he made numerous
genuflections" (M4).

Of all the attitudes of prayer, that which the Christian pre-
fers is praying while standing. The first ecumenical Council in
Nicaea in 325 stipulated that those faithful to the risen Christ
had to celebrate the eucharistic prayer standing: by that action, manifesting that they are already risen from the dead.
Dominic liked to pray standing up. There, simply with his hands
open as a sign of offering, like the one who receives everything, the one who draws the water he needs to live from Jesus'
open side.

When he was at the convent, the holy Father Dominic
also, sometimes, stood before the altar, without holding onto or leaning against anything, his hands held
out in front of his chest, like an open book (M5).

In order to identify himself with his Savior, who offered himself on the cross, Saint Dominic particularly liked to pray with his arms extended in a cross, the palms opened to heaven. We don't say that he had received the Stigmata, like his contemporary Saint Francis. He didn't request that either. But he wanted to fulfill the Lord's invitation to carry his cross in order to be worthy to be called his disciple. "Other times, we also saw the holy Father Dominic pray with his hands open, his arms tightly stretched out in the form of a cross, standing, his body as straight as he could hold it" (M6).

And always in the posture of a man standing up, Saint Dominic adopted a position that was original, swift and straight to his target like an arrow shot by a bow. He was stretched towards the Lord. He threw himself, or rather, he allowed himself to be thrown towards his Lord through the impetus of the Holy Spirit who is the powerful motor of prayer within us.

> We often saw him standing erect, pointing his entire body towards heaven, in the way in which an arrow that is stretched tight in a bow would be shot straight into the blue sky. He raised his tightly outstretched hands over his head, one joined to the other, or just opened as if he was to receive something from heaven (M7).

Dominic is totally plunged into prayer; just like a wine, he is decanted, purified, transformed, and distilled in all of his thoughts, he thrusts himself into it in order to become a perfect offering. It's not so much that he prayed with his body but that his body became prayer. He was the perfect expression of what Saint Paul said: "…but we ourselves, who have the first fruits of the Spirit, groan inwardly while we wait for adoption, the redemption of our bodies" (Rom 8:23). Dominic's groans in his prayers, his various body positions, and even the fact that this prayer continued throughout the night all manifested this work of transformation of the prayer within him. He didn't pray for himself. Like Christ, he prayed for others. He let the Lord inaugurate, in him, this remodeling of the creation that he wanted for the whole world. "We know that the whole creation has been groaning in labor pains until now" (Rom 8:22).

The originality of Dominic's prayer is truly there. His prayer was active, just like his preaching was, for there was really no difference. Prayer is the active nocturnal face of preaching. During the day, the farmer sowed his seeds. At night, the Lord made his seeds grow. During the day, Dominic dedicated himself to man and preaching. He dedicated the nights to God and prayer. One is inseparable from the other, just like modeling clay and its finishing in the kiln. One single and same work, one single and same but coming from one singular preoccupation: the salvation of souls.

REFLECTION QUESTIONS

How do I pray, both formally and informally? Is my formal prayer totally attentive to God in the Mass, God in my presence, God in my heart and soul? How do I sit (or stand) when at prayer? Is my back straight? Is my breathing relaxed? Is my mind free from distraction? Are my physical gestures and postures conducive to attentive praying? Does my formal prayer carry over into my daily life? How aware am I that my dealings with others—my time at work and at leisure—are really opportunities for informal praying?

DAY SIX

A Man of His Word

FOCUS POINT
Dominic always put the Word of God into action. The Word
and action were inseparable; one could not be without the other.
It is an empty life that reads the Word and professes the Word
but does not allow the Word to guide its daily life. The Word is
to be internalized (from reading and listening to the Bible and
consuming the Blessed Sacrament at Mass). After the Word is
internalized, we are transformed and our actions are enliv-
ened and nourished by the Word. Dominic lived his life according to the Word, Jesus Christ, and we are called to do so
too.

The blessed Dominic had a very ardent thirst for the salvation of souls, of which he was an incomparable apostle. He gave himself with such fervor to preaching that he urged and ordered his brothers to proclaim the Word of God day and night, in churches and in homes, through the fields and on the roads, in a word, everywhere, and to speak of nothing but God. He pursued heretics, which he opposed through his preaching, in all the ways that were within his power (VIE, p. 82: testimony of Guillaume Peyre, abbot of the monastery at Saint Paul of Narbonne).

In his particular context, where the Church was organized in *orders*, that is, groups which each have a specific duty (an *office*), Saint Dominic's wanted to give the Church an *order* whose *office* would be to preach the gospel. From his bishop, Don Diego of Osma, he had learned that a preacher of the gospel, if he wanted to truly be evangelical, must be poor. Dominic would give this requirement a permanent and original form.

Like Saint Francis of Assisi wanted to follow the poor Christ as a poor person, Brother Dominic wanted, by preaching, to imitate Christ, the preacher of the gospel. The Word occupied Saint Dominic's daily life. He was inhabited by the Word because he was inhabited by Christ. The Word of God who made himself become man. He spent his nights speaking of others with this Word (Christ). He spent his days speaking of this Word to others.

To his contemporaries, Dominic was a preacher with no equal. Everyone agreed.

Throughout all of the bases of his activities, with all manners of people, he never lacked a word of edification; he abounded with stories that could bring the souls of his listeners to love Christ and despise temporal things. He showed himself everywhere as a man of the gospel, in word and in deed (LIB, no. 104).

The person who wants to learn from him has certainly felt this attraction for the Word of God that Saint Dominic transmitted to his brothers and sisters. And he would love to know one or more of these anecdotes that are passed from one generation to the next: they are Saint Dominic's *fioretti*.

First, there is this one about a meeting with a heretical hotel manager from Toulouse which remains the model for Dominic's apostolic zeal. Here is this anecdote which refers to a time well before Dominic thought about founding his order:

When he discovered that the residents of this territory (Languedoc) had already been heretics for some time, he was greatly moved with compassion for so many souls who were so miserably led astray. During the very night he was staying in the city (of Toulouse), the subprior (Dominic) attacked the heretical host of the house with force and warmth, multiplying the discussions and his own arguments to persuade him. The heretic couldn't resist the wisdom and the spirit he expressed: through the intervention of the divine Spirit, Dominic brought him to the faith (LIB, no. 15).

Brother Dominic was the opposite of a glib speaker. He didn't speak just for the fun of it. If he spoke, it was because he was seized, in the very depth of himself, by the misery of these men

who spoiled their eternal salvation. He knew that only the Word
of God, the authentic Word of God, could save them. Thus, he
must proclaim this Word so that he could do his job.

Right away, Dominic had found what was missing in his
method: the persuasive argument. What is shocking about
Dominic is his boldness. He would go to meet those who
wanted Christ to save them. There was a dual requirement:
the first, to go to those who should hear the Word and, the
second, to be persuaded that proclaiming the Word could be
useful.

He would also come to specialize in a manner that was
very particular: the contradictory debate.

> We instituted a number of disputes (*disputatio* has the
> meaning of a contradictory debate) under the arbitra-
> tion of the deputies from Pamiers, Lavaur, Montréal,
> and Fanjeaux. There, we gathered to attend a discus-
> sion of the faith (LIB, no. 23).

Dominic increased the number of these meetings. He made a
strong impression. Sadly, the details of the jousts have not been
revealed to us. It is simply reported that Brother Dominic won
over his opponents through the strength of his arguments and
by his powers of persuasion. He spoke like someone who is
inhabited by the Word. He had reached this great art, the fruit
of his long nights of contemplation, of letting the Word speak
within him.

Amongst all of these disputes, one has remained particularly famous: that in Fanjeaux in 1207. The exchanges were so
rich, the arguments so strong on both sides, that it was agreed
that each party submit a written report to a commission of
arbitration. "We should consider the beliefs of the party of

which the arbitrators judge the report better founded on reason to be victorious" (LIB, no. 24).

But the arbitrators, in spite of a long debate, did not reach a decision. Instead they chose to declare a sort of "stalemate."

> The idea came to them to throw the two reports into the flames of a fire: if one of them was not consumed, it undoubtedly contained the truth of faith. They then built a great fire: both reports were thrown into it. The heretics' book was quickly consumed. But the other, written by the man of God, Dominic, not only remained intact, but in the presence of everyone, jumped out, far from the flames. Thrown in for a second and a third time, it jumped out each time, openly manifesting to the truth of the faith and the holiness of the one who had written it (LIB, no. 25).

These are means that people today wouldn't dare try. But nevertheless! Why wouldn't God intervene so that the truth is manifested? Again, dare we ask it of him? Furthermore, it isn't sure that the opponents would be converted.

Another anecdote, that of the trip that Brother Dominic made from Paris to Toulouse with Brother Bertrand: as was their custom, they made a detour through the Shrine at Rocamadour in order to pray at the church dedicated to Our Lady. There were some German pilgrims, who, when they heard them praying and singing, joined them. Then, they invited the brothers to share their meal. This lasted for four days.

> One fine day, Dominic sighed to his companion and said: "Brother Bertrand, I truly have a bad conscience; we have well harvested of the earthly goods of these

pilgrims without sowing a single seed of the goods of
the Spirit in them. Please let us pray to the Lord so that
he will give us the ability to understand and speak their
language, so that we can also proclaim the Lord Jesus
to them as well." Having done this, they were able to
speak German in an intelligible way, much to the amaze-
ment of all. They spent an additional four days with them,
speaking to them about the Lord Jesus (EVA, p. 98).

We could give numerous other examples of such *fioretti*, for
there are many. One word is enough to sum up Brother
Dominic's preaching; it is a word that has come to be the motto
of his order: truth. Above all, Saint Dominic wanted the truth
of the gospel to triumph when faced with the errors of heresy.
He gave his life to the service of this truth, for it is not just one
truth amongst others for him, a truth that is subject to being
unreliable, it is the only path that leads to eternal life. We must
not deprive the world of this light.

But the truth is not just in the contents, it is also in the
manner. Dominic spoke truthfully. He was convincing because
there was no difference between what he said and what his
deepest convictions were. Truth was united to his life. Not
only did he not know how to lie, nor twist the truth, but he
spoke with the abundant heart of a child, from which he didn't
know how to have any duplicity.

Finally, Dominic was truth in that he always followed up
what he said by what he did. There is another adage that he
left to his order. He asked that they preach *verbo et exemplo*,
by word and deed.

At the end of this sixth day, we will remember this passage
of a written portrait of Dominic, given to us by Jourdain of
Saxe: "Everywhere, he was known as a man of the gospel, in

word and in deed" (LIB, no. 104). He was a man who put the Word he served into action.

REFLECTION QUESTIONS

How does the Word transform me when I encounter it in my life and during the Mass? How do I respond to the call of the Word? Do I shut it out at times? If so, what obstacles must I overcome so that I am open to the Word at all times? Do I read the Bible regularly? Do I reflect on the words of Scripture and try to see how they apply to situations and relationships in my life? Let me pray that God will grace me with the openness I need to be transformed and nourished by the goodness of his Word.

DAY SEVEN

A Man of Remembrance

FOCUS POINT

Dominic was concerned with the salvation of souls; it was a driving force in his life, and the reason he preached the Word of God. At the center of this mission was liturgy, the Eucharist, the Mass. This is the nourishment that fed Dominic and his community of brothers and sisters. In remembrance of Jesus Christ, his passion and death, his giving himself in sacrifice on our behalf, Dominic held the liturgy and the Mass at the center of his life; it helped to energize him in his preaching and in his service to God.

From the very wishes of Saint Dominic, the solemn and communal celebration of the liturgy must be considered by all to be one of the principal tasks that our vocation requires.... The celebration of the liturgy is the center and the heart of our entire life from which unity especially takes root (LCO, no. 57).

A ll of Saint Dominic's spiritual life was founded on the celebration of the divine liturgy. He drew his inspiration from it during his life in the chapter in Osma, he renewed his taste for it through his visits to the Cistercian monks where he took their habit, not to become a monk, but through a kind of attachment to the way of life that was totally liturgical.

The liturgy is the public expression of the interior divine life of the Church. God could have communicated in many different ways with mankind. He chose the way of incarnation. He used human language, which is based on words and on exchanged signs. Through the liturgy, God is in permanent and tangible contact with mankind. He nourishes them with his proclaimed Word. He shapes them by the sacraments, the source of life. He convenes them for a fraternal meeting. He hears their prayers and answers them.

Saint Dominic founded his order at the heart of the Church. His priests, even though they are not part of the *presbyterium* of the bishop, have a priestly and liturgical ministry. Their preaching is a ministry conferred by the Church. They celebrate the Eucharist, the source, center, and summit of the liturgy. They practice the ministry of the absolution of sins, the liturgy of the renewal of a divine life in a wounded soul. And if they don't regularly, even as pastors, administer the other sacraments, they are entitled to do so.

But beyond all of this, what Saint Dominic left as a legacy to his sisters and brothers was the daily celebration of the Liturgy of the Hours.

He wanted as many sisters as brothers to pray together. Without renouncing indispensable personal prayer, they received the responsibility to assure the permanence of praise and intercession in the Church. He asked them to make this prayer the center and the heart of their religious apostolic life.

He wanted their time to be punctuated by this celebration, even if schedules had to be rearranged in order to allow theological work and preaching, for the era itself had to be evangelized. The liturgy sanctified the years, the weeks, the days, and the hours.

The Dominican sister-monks devoted their entire lives to this liturgical celebration of the Word of God that their brother-monks had the mission to proclaim. Their perseverance to the Liturgy of the Hours and the importance they accorded to this celebration came from Saint Dominic himself. Through them, they actively participate in the goal of the order which is the salvation of souls.

Their brothers nourish themselves with the psalms and this gospel they are proclaiming. Their Constitution explains:

In the liturgy, above all in the Eucharist, the mystery of salvation is made present through and in which the brothers have a share, that they contemplate and proclaim to mankind through their preaching so that it will be incorporated with Christ through the sacraments of faith.

In the liturgy, united to Christ, the brothers glorify God for his will's eternal plan and the admirable gift of his grace; they invoke the Father of mercy for the

universal Church and for the needs and salvation of
the entire world. That is why the celebration of the
liturgy is the center and the heart of our entire life from
which unity especially takes root (LCO, no. 57).

This reminds us that the liturgy permeates the entire life of the
brothers. Their very life is liturgical; it must say, in all aspects,
that the Lord is celebrated. The rites of the table, fraternal
relationships, the procedures of the chapters, and even their
silence form the liturgical cloth of the life of the preachers.

The first Constitutions of the order retain a trace where
we can sense the personal touch of Saint Dominic.

Our brothers must remain together for the matins,
Mass, and all of the canonical hours; and even to have
their meals, unless the superior wants otherwise. All of
the hours must be recited in the church in a brief and
strict fashion, in such a way that the brothers do not
lose their devotion and that their studies do not suffer
in any way. This is how we must do this: we will observe a rhythm in the midst of the verse with a pause,
without prolonging the voice either at the pause or at
the end of the verse; but just as we said, to end in a
way that is both brief and strict. We observe this according to the liturgical time (VIE, pp. 165–166).

From this text, we can take note of several things:

1. Contrary to what monks do, above all in Saint Dominic's
   time, the brother preachers did not pass the majority of
   their time in church. They were either involved in preaching or in studies which prepared them for preaching. There

was a hierarchy. In as much as he attached importance to the liturgical recitation of the Liturgy of the Hours, Dominic put the office in its place, which is certainly not secondary, but second.

2. The dispensation that Saint Dominic wanted was not a simple clause of mercy for the brothers who were too ill to go down to the church, it was truly an indispensable tool for the life of a preacher. Any brother could be excused from the public recitation of the Liturgy of the Hours (but not from the private one, if he is a priest) by reason of preaching duties or studies.

3. The precision with respect to a recitation of the Liturgy of the Hours is strict and brief, with a double goal, precisely: on the one hand to not lose devotion, on the other to not obstruct either preaching and studies.

4. Meals and liturgies must be had together. Community life characterizes the life of the sons of Saint Dominic.

"Do this in remembrance of me," said the Lord. Thus, Saint Dominic, in imitation of the apostles, was a man who served through remembrance. Remembrance is not a memory. To remember a memory brings one back to a past event. There are events, situations, and people who have marked those who were present to them. They remember them as a memory. They bring them back to memory. They keep them nostalgically, or, to the contrary, they give them a bad memory.

But here, we speak of a remembrance. It is necessary to actualize events which remain contemporary across all generations. Today, for me, I now see that Christ was born, was betrayed, suffers, dies, and rises from death. Today, this instant, aims to show me that Christ gives his body and his sacramental blood to me in Communion. Today I hear the Word of

God proclaimed "as if I was there," and this Word of God touches me. It touches me in the physical meaning of the term. Dominic, through his vocation as a preacher, received this grace of the actualization of the salvific action of the Lord, as much in his preaching as in his life. With all of those who participate in the divine liturgy, whether as a preacher and celebrant or as a faithful reader and by receiving Communion, they put into action the commandment of the Lord: "Do this in remembrance of me."

REFLECTION QUESTIONS

Does liturgy, the Mass, and the Eucharist energize me the way it did Dominic? Is liturgy a regular, routine part of my life? If not, how can I bring that energizing and nourishing element into my life? Might I considering praying the Liturgy of the Hours three times a day, in step with the Church all over the world? Perhaps this will help me to incorporate regular liturgy into my daily life so that my prayer life and life outside of formal prayer becomes more united.

A Man of Government

FOCUS POINT

Dominic lived his life with an unwavering dedication to the truth, and governed his order by the same method. Dominic's relationship with God made for a strong foundation as he constructed the governing model of his order. The members of his order had great trust in Dominic because, like the law of God, Dominic never wavered in his commitment to the truth. Although Dominic was rigid in his allegiance to the truth, he was flexible in allowing for the freedom of the members of his order by respecting the gifts and talents given them by God.

It was thus that after the celebration of the Council, they (Dominic and his bishop) returned and told the brothers the pope's answer. Soon after, they, the future preachers, made a profession to the Rule of Saint Augustine, that eminent preacher. Furthermore, they imposed some additional practices of strict observance regarding kinds of food, fasting, sleep, and the wearing of wool. They resolved and instituted to not have any material goods so that the bother of temporal affairs did not present an obstacle to the ministry of preaching. They decided to only have revenue (LIB, no. 42).

It appeared to be a good idea (to Saint Dominic) to elect a brother to be an abbot who would have authority over the other brothers, like a superior or a leader. He would have the power of control. Thus, Brother Matthew was canonically elected as the abbot. In this order, he was the first and last to carry the title abbot, for the brothers later decided, as a means to underline their humility, that the one who would head the order would not be called abbot, but master (LIB, no. 48).

A man of prayer, a man of his word, Saint Dominic was also a man of government. He knew how to lead because he knew how to be obedient. He knew how to make decisions, for he knew how to let things reach their maturity. He knew how to organize because he knew how to withstand the rigors of the land.

Saint Dominic was first obedient in his youth when he followed his bishop. He was also obedient to events, allowing himself to be guided by them and finding, in them, the expression of the will of God. Later on, he was obedient to his brothers when he bent to their refusal to comply.

So that the brothers apply themselves with more energy to study and preaching, Brother Dominic wanted the illiterate lay brothers of his order to govern over those who were educated in those things which applied to the administration and maintenance of temporal things (VIE, p. 53, deposition of Brother Jean d'Espagne).

In him, obedience shaped the interior man. In his relationship with God, as in matters of charity, he renounced all personal will. He did not do anything for his own ends. But his spiritual disposition did not hinder him from being a man of government, one who knew how to lead when necessary. The older brothers emotionally remembered Brother Dominic's decision, on August 15, 1217, when the order had just been confirmed, and he sent his brothers away. Objections arose from amidst the brothers as well as with their friends and protectors. But Master Dominic held firm. The following is what Brother Jean d'Espagne tells us, because, for him, the memory was bitter, since he refused to go on the road without a little money to the point of forcing Saint Dominic to give in to him (see EVA, p. 92):

When the witness (that is, he, himself) was at the Saint Romanus convent in Toulouse with Brother Dominic, the latter, against the better judgment of the brother, sent him to Paris with five clerical brothers and one lay brother, to study, preach, and found a convent there. He told them not to worry, that everything would work out: "Don't go against me; I know what I'm doing" (VIE, p. 52).

This phrase has remained famous for the brothers. Taken as if it was coming from a saint, it doesn't appear to be an expression of gratuitous authority, but just the opposite, as the manifestation of a profound spiritual life that results in a clear decision. Dominic acts like a man whose driving force is his charisma as a founder. If he hadn't had this inspiration, this prophetic vision of the future, his order wouldn't have lasted.

What is striking about the important decisions that punctuate Saint Dominic's life, from the time when he wasn't only just a preacher of the gospel, but the founder of an order devoted to preaching, is that he never acted for himself, but always as a function of either a firm goal or the common good. He disappeared behind his decision. He didn't act on a whim, or in the passion of the moment. His decision was beyond him. He acted as if he was controlled by a will that was stronger than his own and which led him to where his order should go.

This inspiration, doubtlessly founded upon a gifted nature, would bring the most durable fruit into the institution that it would put into action.

Master Dominic dedicated the final years of his life to equip his order with institutional bases that were sufficiently clear and precise so that his successors could efficiently legislate. During the two general chapters (1220 and 1221), important decisions were made which the order has not changed since, and particularly regarding the institution of definers, "Who would have the authority over other brothers and the entire chapter, with the power to decree, define, and rule for the duration of the chapter" (VIE, p. 59).

The first general chapter of the order was celebrated in Bologna. This witness was present. It fell on the blessed Brother Dominic to enact the institution of definers who would have full power over the entire order, over the master and even over the definers themselves: they could define, decree, rule, and punish, contingent upon the respect of the authority due to the master (VIE, p. 36; testimony of Brother Venture of Verona).

We can also give Saint Dominic credit for this wise decision; that a law could only be definitively admitted or abolished if decided in three successive chapters: "To avoid duplication of Constitutions, we agree to decree nothing without having it approved by two successive chapters: at the third, that is, the one which follows immediately, we can confirm or negate this disposition..." (VIE, pp. 182–183).

This genius of organization that permitted his order to withstand the centuries by adapting to diverse cultures, by handling crises and resisting the passage of time, was accompanied by great practical wisdom. Master Dominic was the opposite of a systematic spirit. He knew the importance of good legislation, but he also knew its limitations.

In order to be a man of government, one must combine knowledge with a good practice of the laws which are the guardians of the freedoms of both the individuals as well as groups. But one must also know how to lead men so that they give the best of themselves. Saint Dominic had all of these qualities. He was the founder of his order which, by withstanding the passage of time, shows the solidity of his institution. He was the uncontested master of the first generation of religious sisters and brothers. Many founders of other religious orders had to suffer at the hands of their brothers and sisters, many even were rejected by their own foundations or forgotten over the years. Saint Dominic, who was honored by all until the end of his life, has left a souvenir that many men of government would envy. One knew that he could count on him: he never contradicted himself, or changed his word from one person to another. Nothing is more precious than knowing that the person who is leading you will not change his ideas, even if the political wind changes. Also, he was loved with a love that was filled with respect, at times with veneration, that we could have for a leader, when he is a true leader.

REFLECTION QUESTIONS

In what ways do I govern those people who look up to me in my life? Do I model for them a person of strong moral mettle, a person who does not waver in his/her dedication to the truth of the Lord? In what ways do I try to help guide others in their own faith lives? Do I pay close attention to their talents and God-given gifts so that I might be wise to direct them to serve God according to the gifts he has given them? How might I take a more active role of leadership in my parish community or in my own family?

DAY NINE

A Man of Intelligence

FOCUS POINT

In our lives of service to God, we are called to use every faculty
given us by our Lord so that we may serve him to our capacity.
Dominic recognized this responsibility of service, and empha-
sized the importance of study in his life as well as in the lives of
the members of his order. Dominic loved to preach the gospel,
but it was his intense study of the gospel that served as his
foundation for preaching it. For Dominic, the gospel was not
so much a text as a person. By reading and studying and devel-
oping a relationship with the Word of God, Dominic deep-
ened his relationship with Jesus, and proclaimed the Word with
greater authority and passion. We are all called to do the same.

Our father, Saint Dominic, had yet another way to pray, one that is filled with beauty, devotion, and charm. He devoted himself to it after the canonical hours and after the communal thanksgiving that followed the meal. This good father, admirable and overflowing with the spirit of devotion, which he had drawn from the divine words that were sung in the choir or refectory, quickly stole away to a solitary place, in a cell or elsewhere, in order to read and pray, concentrated completely within himself and fixed upon God. Peacefully, he sat himself down and, after having made the Sign of the Cross, read from whatever book was before him: his soul then experienced a gentle emotion, as if he had heard the Lord himself speak to him (M8).

I t was from the gospel that Saint Dominic drew the ardor for his preaching. He had received it from his predecessors, transmitted it to his brothers and sisters, and practiced it through *lectio divina*. The tireless preacher of the gospel was also a fervent reader of the gospels. For there was but one Word of God. The same one that must be proclaimed from the rooftops must also be sung in the choir, read and meditated in prayer, contemplated in preaching, and shared in fraternal life.

We say that Saint Dominic did not leave a treatise of devotion, nor a manual of spiritual exercises. But by adding up all of the elements that constituted his interior armature, we discover that what was left was better than a methodology; he left a practice. In order to follow him, we must imitate him. He could have said, just as Saint Paul did: "Be imitators of me, as I am of Christ" (1 Cor 11:1).

The Blessed Jean of Fiesole (known to us as Fra Angelico)

has left us, in the cells of the convent at Saint Mark of Florence, an admirable illustration. In it, we see Saint Dominic seated and reading. His face is young, for it reflects the eternal youth of the text upon which he is meditating. We sense that he is concentrating on his text, absorbed by it. This attitude is the same as the one described again in this eighth manner of prayer, which goes on to describe Dominic as he is reading:

> When he argued with a companion, at times he appeared to be unable to contain his words and thoughts, and at times to pleasantly listen, discuss, and battle. We saw him laugh and cry, one after another, fix his gaze and lower his eyes, then speak to himself quietly and hit his chest (M8).

In other words, when he read the Scriptures, and especially the gospel, our father, Saint Dominic, truly dedicated himself to his reading! He dedicated himself to it just as he did to someone who spoke to him. Everyone said that he paid particular special attention to people. For him, the gospel was not so much a text as a person.

In the same way as he met Christ in each person to whom he had proclaimed the gospel, he met the Lord in person each time he meditated upon his gospel. It was also his custom to "quickly go from reading to prayer and then from prayer to contemplation." Such is his method. It is the simplest of all. It was that very one the Lord used when he walked with Cleopas and his companion on the road that went from Jerusalem to Emmaus. What did he do? "He interpreted to them the things about himself in all the scriptures" (Lk 24:27). And Dominic, just like all of those who imitate him by practicing divine reading, can say, when they lift their eyes up from their book and walk as beggars on the path: "Were not our hearts burning within us while he was talking to us on the road, while he was opening the scriptures to us?" (Lk 24:32).

Dominic was not assailed as we are by mountains of paperwork that we must read each day. He was not overwhelmed under the weight of books, each more indispensable than the next. In fact, he had few books. According to his brothers, those who traveled the long trips with him, he traveled with a few books and used the time spent along the route to meditate at length about the teachings.

> Verbally, or in letters, Brother Dominic urged his brothers in the order to study, without relenting, both the Old and New Testaments...he always carried the Gospel of Saint Matthew and Saint Paul's epistles, studying them so much that he practically knew them by heart (VIE, p. 55).

One could only imagine what this contact with these words of the Lord meant to this man. He didn't hesitate to express his interior feelings, as we have seen in various examples of his interactions with his brothers. "And when he was reading, he venerated his book; bending down to it, kissing it with affection, especially when it was the gospel and when he had read the words that Jesus Christ had deemed him worthy to pronounce from his mouth."

Isn't this just like a lover does when he receives a love letter, reading and re-reading it with passion, considering that this letter is a manifestation of that person's presence? Dominic was not one to put the authenticity of the word of Christ into question.

FROM READING TO STUDYING

In his youth, Saint Dominic had received a solid theological education. His biographer stated:

> He spent four years in religious education. Such was his perseverance and his avid desire to draw from the waters of the holy Scriptures, he was tireless when he studied. He spent many nights with practically no sleep, yet in the depth of his spirit, his tenacious memory retained the truth that he received from his ears. And what he learned with ease, thanks to these gifts, he watered with feelings of his piety and made them sprout with salvific works (LIB, no. 7).

In his later years, Dominic, too busy with his preaching, vigils, and the concerns for the institution of his order, did not have the leisure time to do theological work. But he always remained concerned with studying, as much for himself as for his first friars.

Theological work, which is, above all, a work of faith in the service of proclaiming the gospel, will, then, be an essential aspect of the life of someone who wants to follow and learn from Saint Dominic. He will know how to go directly from reading to meditation to contemplation to theology and then to preaching.

In the service of this diligent intellectual work, Saint Dominic instituted two new, but necessary, practices in order to favor study: the *dispensing* of the public recitation of the Liturgy of the Hours (which allowed the brothers to give their maximum to their work) and the *cells* (which permitted these brothers to work better and more efficiently). In the cells, those who wanted to could study, write, pray, sleep, and even sit vigil during the night for their studies (see LIB, no. 44).

Saint Dominic didn't necessarily want to found an order of intellectuals, but he gave intelligence an important place. His brothers followed in his footsteps in this manner.

REFLECTION QUESTIONS

In what ways do I develop my understanding of God and his Word through study? Do I read the Bible, the Catechism of the Catholic Church, or a Bible study aid with regularity? Have I thought about joining or starting up a Bible study group in my parish or neighborhood? What would be some informative and interesting resources for my study of God and his Word? Might I ask a priest or religious what they might recommend or perhaps visit my local religious bookstore for further investigation?

DAY TEN

A Man of Experience

FOCUS POINT

No one exists in a vacuum, separated from the rest of the world. We are a gregarious people, called to be with one another in work, play, and prayer. Dominic knew this all too well. He knew life in community to be hard work, full of sacrifice, but also full of joy. What better way to give one's self in service to the Lord than by giving one's self in service to a brother. Self-sacrifice is a way of life in a community of brothers and sisters. In our own lives, we feel a similar call. And though we may not live in a religious community, we do live in a familial and societal setting, and this affords us great opportunities for service and sacrifice.

*Why are you gathered if it's not to live together in unanimity,
making only one single heart and soul in God? (...) For you,
everything will be in common (Rule of Saint Augustine).*

*Just as we are told by the rule, our first reason for being
gathered in a community is to live together and to have one
single soul and one single heart in God (LCO, no. 2).*

*Just as in the Church of the apostles, amongst us the com-
munion is founded, built, and affirmed in the same Spirit: in
him, we receive the Word of God the Father, in the same faith,
we contemplate him with the same heart and we praise him
with the same voice; in him, we form a single body, we share
the same bread; finally, in him, we have everything in common
and are all destined for the same evangelization (LCO, no. 3).*

Without question, Saint Dominic's order was founded
on community life. By choosing Saint Augustine's rule,
which was, itself, founded on the first Christians' model of the
Church in Jerusalem, and by speaking in the first Constitutions about the necessity for unanimity in the communal life,
Saint Dominic put the emphasis on what was essential: the
vita apostolica, that is, the life of the apostles.

It is true that Saint Dominic's era was far from the time of
the individualists. In the thirteenth century, the thinking was
not the same as it was in the sixteenth with respect to the individual, his personal conscience and destiny. To the contrary,
the thinking was with respect to the community, everything in
common, like the communion of saints.

In the religious traditions that preceded it and from which
we draw, everything was communal. Everyone had the aim to
realize the ideal of Christian life that is described in the Acts of

the Apostles: "They had only one single heart and one single soul and they put all of their goods in common" (4:32).

When Dominic received the inspiration to found an order of preachers, he automatically thought "community." He wanted brothers that would live together, pray together, and preach together.

Furthermore, in the chronicles, we always see Dominic in the midst of his brothers. He is never alone. That would be inconceivable. He worked in the midst of the communities that were founded, little by little. And when he traveled, he went from convent to convent, adopting the local customs (cooking and prayer). Even along the route, he was never alone, always with one or more companions. It is these people who give us the most precious testimonies with respect to Brother Dominic's attitude in various circumstances. For communal life was no easier than it is today. The adage remains true: *vita communis, maxima paenitentia* (communal life is the greatest of all punishments).

Dominic is described as having all of the qualities necessary to lead a communal life:

> He was a man who was humble, gentle, patient, kind, quiet, peaceful, sober, modest, pious, fully mature in all of his actions and words, a consoler for all and above all, for his brothers, an incomparable promoter for the religious life, an incomparable lover of poverty, and so forth (VIE, p. 46).

Today, we could say that Saint Dominic had a charisma for spiritual accompaniment. He was not happy just to draw brothers to his order, he knew how to accompany them, support them in their difficult times, to defend them when the inevitable temptations in life come, stimulate them when they lose their courage, and reprimand them when necessary. For Saint Dominic did not lack this courage, so rare in the communal life, to know how to admonish sinners without hurting them. In him, we recognize a certain rigor, just but severe, as Brother Frogier of Penna relates:

> Just as he observed the rule rigorously and to its fullest extent, he required the same faithfulness on the part of the brothers. If he came to discover that some of them had transgressed, he punished them; but with such a gentleness, and with words that were so sweet that no one was offended, even if the punishment had been very harsh (VIE, p. 73).

For Saint Dominic, the communal life was not limited to co-habitation in the same building. It was necessary, so that it would work, to have the indispensable element of unanimity. In the first place, to have only one soul. Not only in the ordinary communal life, which is already not so easy, but also in the taking charge of this communal life. Just like his Cistercian friends lead a monastic life, from arising to going to bed, that is integrally communal, Brother Dominic wanted his brothers to lead a no less communal life, but the life of apostles. The adage that presides over this organization is: *that which has to be lived by all, must be decided by all.*

The Dominican communal life is one that has been studied by many chapters. Normally, a brother never lives alone. He lives in a convent, which is another word to express in communion. The convent regularly meets in a chapter. Everything is decided there. Convents are also gathered into provinces. Each province has its own chapter which must decide what concerns it. And all of the provinces must meet once every three years in a general chapter which has the power to decide everything (except changing the essentials of the Dominican vocation).

Everything must be decided unanimously. Without it, the meetings would become juxtapositions of individuals defending corporate decisions like we see in numerous gatherings that we label as being democratic. Without unanimity, there is no longer community, but collectives. There is nothing such as this in what Saint Dominic had in mind, nor in his project. His genius was to have seen, right from the start, the dangers of this communal government and to have granted it the means so that it stays communal and governable.

His contemporaries were certain that everything in his order rested on the prayer of its founder. Today, his brothers are still convinced of it: "He helps his missionaries through the intercession of his prayers, and the power of the Lord works to increase them" (LIB, no. 62).

All those who are followers know this: the communal life only works if the price is paid. And this price consists of giving the entirety of oneself, to no longer belong to oneself, to give of oneself to others without expectation. That is as true for the daily life in the convents, as it is in the apostolic life. It is also to be poor, in the spirit of Saint Dominic, to retain nothing for oneself, to give all that one has received, to live in total dependence on his brothers as benefactors, trusting in the evangelical logic of losing everything in order to gain everything.

A great determination and strength of soul is necessary, just like Saint Dominic had.

But the communal life, when it is lived as it should be, is the finest source of happiness—this happiness that is promised by the Lord and that the world can't understand. The following testimony from the blessed Brother Reginald expresses what many other brothers could say:

> I remember that while he was still living, Brother Matthew who had known him, glorious and difficult in his delicacy, asked Brother Reginald with astonishment: "Don't you feel a certain repugnance, Master, at this habit you have chosen?" But he, lowering his head, replied: "I believe I don't deserve to live in this order, for I find too much happiness here" (LIB, no. 64).

REFLECTION QUESTIONS

In what ways does my self-sacrifice manifest itself in my familial and church-going life? How does this self-sacrifice bring me more in touch with the gospel message? Am I aware of the continuous abundance of opportunities to serve God and my fellow brothers and sisters in my daily life by living out the gospel message of service and self-sacrifice? Do I feel the deepening of my relationship with God as I give more and more of myself to others in humble service and love? What further opportunities are available in my parish so that I might expand this call to serve?

DAY ELEVEN

A Man of the Cross

FOCUS POINT

It is said that saints are most in tune with their sinfulness and the sinfulness of the world. They are, like Dominic, so close to the Lord that they feel his great pain at this sinful world, and are pained to the deepest parts of their being as well. Dominic suffered with the Lord because he united himself with the one who united God and mankind. Jesus Christ, in his passion, gave himself totally to the Father for love of us; Dominic follows this path, seeking the suffering of the passion as a path to deeper union to and an expression of love for Jesus Christ.

Saint Dominic also stood before the altar. There, his gaze fixed on the crucifix, he contemplated it with incomparable penetration. Before it, he made numerous genuflections. Occa-

sionally, as well, from compline until the middle of the night,
sometimes he stood up, and at other times, he genuflected.
Our father, Saint Dominic, came to have a great feeling of
confidence in God's mercy for himself, for all sinners, and for
the preservation of the younger brothers he sent out to the
world to preach the gospel (M5).

▬▬▬▬▬

S aint Dominic's prayer tends to be united with Christ's
prayer. It becomes identified with the passion of the Lord
Jesus: his passion for his Father, his passion for the salvation
of mankind, his loving passion and his painful passion. The
summit of Jesus' prayer is his prayer on the cross, this prayer
about which we only know a few fragments, a few cries, but
about which we can assume is filled with immeasurable love.
Dominic had the grace to perceive something from Jesus' prayer
of agony. His sons and daughters are invited to participate in
this grace of communion with Jesus' sacrifice. For this sacrifice does not come freely. It is the price that is paid for the
salvation of souls. Not the price that God requires, but the
price that each of us should pay in order to show what part
one is willing to play in God's concern to save all mankind.

Jesus took the best part. It will not be taken away from
him. The martyrs who received the grace to shed their blood
like their Lord come next. That is why Brother Dominic wanted
to be a martyr. He did not want it for himself. He was not
concerned with that. But he wanted to go all the way to the
gift of his own life. He wanted the love within him to bring
fruit worthy of the love that God, himself, manifested for the
poor creatures that we are. "Let the same mind be in you that
was in Christ Jesus" (Phil 2:5).

If the whole world doesn't have the grace to be called to an authentic martyrdom, at least each of us could, in as much as one is called to, approach this ideal, even if it would only be through the desire for it. "He stood up and punished himself with an iron chain, saying: your discipline corrected me until the end (see Ps 18)" (M3).

To us, it seems rather strange that someone could subject himself to such punishments. We see it as a sign of an unbalanced psyche, and in certain cases, this could be true. But for Saint Dominic, it was something altogether different. Through this practice, he manifested the realism of his faith. When he read that Jesus had been beaten by the soldiers, he didn't turn the page to see what came next. He stopped there. He didn't find that to be normal, nor could he tolerate it. He didn't know how to get used to it. He took it for himself. He didn't see why he, a sinner, would not submit himself to that which the one who was innocence itself did. We could perhaps find this practice a little extreme and not feel moved to go this far. But we must be careful to not too quickly treat those people who have the heart to live closer to the passion of Jesus as fools. "The blessed one always wore an iron chain around his waist, right on his flesh; he kept it until he died" (VIE, p. 57).

Here is another detail that we say comes from another era. But what does the man of today do in order to participate in the passion of the Lord, to carry, in his flesh, the suffering and death of Jesus, to try to manifest that he wants to love him as he was loved?

Dominic, in the manner of the great mystics, received the grace to perceive the horror of sin. And he threw his cry into the night that was so often heard by his brothers: "My God, my mercy, what will become of the sinners?" This was not to moan about the evils of the times, but because he saw this gulf that separates the sinner from God. And he could not accept that.

Then, there he was, laying face-down on the ground. He cried, like Jesus cried. "Often, the blessed Dominic prayed while he was completely stretched out, face-down on the ground. In his heart, then, he had true feelings of solemnity. He remembered the teachings of the divine Scriptures, sometimes declaring, in a voice that was loud enough to be heard, this word of the gospel: 'God, be merciful to me, a sinner!' (Lk 18:13). Then he cried and wailed."

These were not just "showy" moans, said just to be heard, but the overflowing of a wounded heart. He had been touched at the most sensitive point of his apostle's soul. That is the solemnity. And he was not crying only about his own sins, but about the sins of the world, about indifference, contempt, and hate for what God represents. And even if we don't have any sin, we must not forget the sins of the world. The following is what he taught the young brothers:

> He urged the youngest ones in these terms: "If you can't cry for your sins because you don't have any, think about the great number of sinners who could be prepared for mercy and charity. For them, Jesus, who penetrated them with his gaze, cried painfully. It was for this reason that the holy King David was crying when he shouted: 'I look at the faithless with disgust, because they do not keep your commands (Ps 119:158)'" (M2).

In other circumstances that were more delicate when he had to intercede for a serious and difficult reason, Saint Dominic used another method. And that one, although he did not prohibit the brothers from using it, he didn't recommend either. It was the method of prayer with the arms extended like a cross. This was not an exercise, but an imitation of the Lord Jesus, an identification with him.

> Other times, we saw the holy Father Dominic praying with his hands open, his arms stretched out tightly in the form of a cross, standing, with his body held as straight as he could. This was how he prayed when, upon his prayer, God resuscitated the young Napoleon, in the sacristy of the convent of Saint Sixte in Rome. He prayed similarly when, near Toulouse, he saved some English pilgrims who were in danger of drowning in the river (M6).

In other circumstances, Brother Dominic, pressed by an emergency, and, in particular, when he prayed for the order that he was in the process of founding, adopted another attitude. He stood up as straight as he could, pointing his body to heaven, like an arrow that had been held in a great bow. He lifted his arms over his head, joining his hands together.

And what did the father ask for his children? Certainly not for human success, but that they would be happy by leading their religious lives without omitting anything. He asked that:

> We judge ourselves as happy through the rigors of poverty, the bitterness of pain, the violence of persecution, the hunger and thirst for justice, the grip of mercy, and that we keep ourselves in a state of joyous fervor, for the observance and practice of the evangelical councils (M7).

After praying this prayer, he was stronger and more serene to address the brothers, to correct those who needed it, to urge or stimulate those who have need for that and for giving advice or making a decision.

It is not surprising that his contemporaries saw him as a prophet.

Saint Dominic, a man of the cross, drew his spiritual energy, above all, from the celebration of the Eucharist. It was there that he could most perfectly commune with the passion of love of his Savior. Brother Étienne could attest to that because:

> Quite often he attended Brother Dominic's Mass and he always saw his eyes and face flooded with tears. Brother Dominic offered the holy sacrifice and said the dominical prayer with such fervor that his devotion was visible to the eyes of his assistants. Brother Étienne does not remember ever having seen him celebrate Mass when he didn't have abundant tears flowing (VIE, p. 64).

Dominic's tears manifested his great mercy. We must not see this as sentimentality in one who is nothing but extreme compassion; a heart of flesh suffering with his humbled God, carrying the cross with his condemned Savior, crying with the sinner who has been broken by his sins. Each of his tears is the drop of water that the priest mixes with the wine in the chalice for the sacrifice of the Mass. Such a small thing, a simple drop of water mixed with the blood of Christ. Really, a little nothing that man could do, to mix his love with the love of his Savior.

REFLECTION QUESTIONS

Do I seek to unite my suffering with that of Jesus Christ's in his passion? Do I recognize the great opportunity to experience this unity in the holy sacrifice of the Mass? How am I affected by my sinfulness? By the sinfulness of the world? Does this sinfulness pain me? If I am presently not able to do this, how can I change my perception of this pain as something that can bring me closer to God rather than something that seems to separate me from my Savior?

DAY TWELVE

A Man of Mary

FOCUS POINT

Mary brought the Word (Jesus) to the world. Jesus proclaimed the Good News; preachers of the past, of today, and of the future continue to spread the gospel message. In the same way that Mary carried the Word inside her, gave birth to him, and cared for him as a mother, Mary is patroness of and mother to all who live, love, and preach the Word of God. As she guided her son, so she guides us, interceding on our behalf, bringing us graces given her by her son for our benefit. Like Dominic, we are called to extend our devotion to her in prayer, specifically by praying the rosary.

Master Reginald was healed of his serious illness and saved from certain dire peril, but not without the miraculous intervention of the divine power. For the Virgin Mary, Queen of heaven, the Mother of mercy, came to him in a visible form in the midst of the ardors of his fever and, with a healing ointment that she carried with her, rubbed his eyes, nostrils, ears, mouth, navel, hands, and feet, adding these words: "I anoint your feet with holy oil so that they will be ready to proclaim the gospel of peace" (Eph 6:15). Furthermore, she made him see the entire habit of our order. Soon, he found himself to be healed and so suddenly restored that the doctors, who had almost been without hope with respect to his recovery, were amazed to attest to signs of a complete healing. Following this, Master Dominic made this remarkable healing known publicly to many people who are still alive. I, myself, recently attended a spiritual conference in Paris where he related it to many people (LIB, no. 57).

R ight from the origins of the order, Saint Dominic had been connected to the Virgin Mary. And even Jourdain of Saxe, his contemporary, successor, and the author of the story we have just read above, assures us that the habit of the order had been revealed by Mary. Another venerable tradition holds that Saint Dominic received, from the hands of the Virgin, the rosary, which his brothers would zealously promote. There are countless churches in which we find either a painting, an altar, or a chapel that illustrates this episode. We see Saint Dominic kneeling before the Virgin Mary who is seated on her throne of glory, holding the infant Jesus on her knees and giving Saint Dominic, often depicted as accompanied by Saint Catherine of Siena, a great rosary. The episode is no less significant, even if it is contested by the historians.

For a man like Dominic, attached as he was to the reality of the Incarnation of the Word of God, devotion to Mary flows from the source. Was it not from her that the Word was made flesh? Was she not the first and best witness to the reality of the events that founded the faith of Christians?

That having been said, we have few testimonies of the presence of Mary in the preaching or prayer of Saint Dominic. We see her appear, on occasion, and, above all, in the recitations of edification. The following is one such example:

> Once, the blessed Dominic, having spent the first part of the night in prayer in the Church, left it at midnight, and went to the dormitory, and, a short while later, began to pray at one end of it. During his prayer, looking at the other end of the dormitory, he saw three beautiful ladies appear; the one in the middle appeared to be a Lady of distinction, more beautiful and dignified than the others. One of her companions was carrying a very brilliant and beautiful vase, the other an aspergillum, which she presented to her. And the lady sprinkled the brothers and traced the Sign of the Cross on them. (...) Prostrating himself (Dominic) at her feet, he begged her to deem to tell him who she was, even though he already knew. At that time, this devout antiphon, *Salve Regina*, was not sung at the convent of the brothers and sisters in Rome; we only read it when we were kneeling. The lady then replied to the blessed Dominic: "I am the one who you invoke every night, and when you say *eia ergo advocata nostra*,

I prostrate myself before my son for the preservation of this order" (VIE, p. 114).

The tradition of singing the *Salve Regina*, every night and at the end of the Liturgy of the Hours (compline) which ends the day on an ultimate prayer, is, itself, certified by the same Jourdain. It is interesting to note that after having said all that he had to say about the life of Saint Dominic, he added "a few other events" that showed his holiness after his death. Amongst others, how a certain Brother Bernard of Bologna was delivered from his terrible temptations:

> This trial that was so cruel for Brother Bernard was the occasion when we pushed to institute the signing of the antiphony *Salve Regina*, after compline in Bologna. The rite stretched from this house to the whole province of Lombardy; finally, the pious and salutary custom was affirmed in the entire order. How many people have been led to tears by the holy praise of the venerable mother of Christ! How many people amongst them who sung it or heard it have felt their affections purified, their hardness softened, and their hearts filled with an ardor of religious love! Do you not believe that the mother of the Redeemer finds her delight in this praise, and is charmed by it? A religious man, worthy of faith told me that he often saw, in spirit, the mother of the Lord, herself, prostrated in the presence of her son and begging him for the preservation of this order the entire time when the brothers were singing: "eia ergo advocata nostra" (LIB, no. 120).

No matter what we think about the reality of these accounts, we could, at least, receive them as testimonials that attest to the Marian devotion in Saint Dominic's era. Incontestably, Dominic and his first brothers loved and venerated the Virgin Mary. They spoke to her as their mother in heaven. They sang her praises; they entrusted her with their ministry and the souls who came to them; they relied upon her effective prayer, for they took it as a "given" that they would get what they asked of her with fervor.

There is nothing astonishing in this, for Mary is, above all, the one who brings the Word to the world. She is the patroness of preachers. It is not without significance that she was with the apostles on Pentecost. She is present to this irruption of the Spirit who would unbind the tongues of the apostles, she who, in a past time, had received the Holy Spirit who made the Word of God grow within her. Mary did not receive the vocation to preach, to found churches, or to speak as a witness. But she has the vocation to protect those who have these missions. She watches over them. She maintains the sacred fires in their hearts.

And when the brothers and sisters of Saint Dominic endlessly meditate on the mysteries of the rosary, they flood themselves with the mysteries of Christ that they deepen with Mary, she who "pondered them in her heart" (Lk 2:19).

Those who want to follow in Dominic's footsteps will find the greatest spiritual joy and consolation in this devotion to the Virgin Mary. Those who must submit themselves to studies that are sometimes austere, whose integrity is questioned, who receive trials, and experience more failures than successes in their ministry, will always find the maternal comfort they need in Mary.

REFLECTION QUESTIONS

Is Mary a significant part of my prayer life? If not, why? Do I recognize the great love that Mary has for me? Do I recognize the desire and willingness she possesses to intercede on my behalf? Have I considered joining a rosary group or praying the rosary nightly on my own? Have I considered fostering a relationship with Mary by other means, perhaps by reading spiritual works (by such authors as Saint Alphonsus Liguori and Saint Louis de Montfort) devoted to the Blessed Virgin?

DAY THIRTEEN

A Man on the Road

FOCUS POINT

All of us are "on the road," to some extent. We move from place to place, encountering strangers and people we know along the way. When we are on the move, are we so hurried that we cannot take the time to listen to someone who is in need of our love and attention? When we go from place to place, we must always be aware of the great opportunities we have to preach the Good News, to spread the gospel message to everyone we meet. When we do this, we are doing that which God calls us to do (share his love with others through us, his instruments), even though the fruits of these labors may never be seen by our eyes.

Brother Dominic always practiced his devotions when he traveled from one country to another, even when he found himself in some distant region. His entire joy was to give himself to his meditations and to return to his contemplations. As he continued along, he would sometimes say to a companion: "It is written in the prophet Hosea: 'I will lead my spouse to the desert and speak to her heart.'" He would also stay separated from his companion, either going ahead of him or following him at a distance. Thus, he continued alone and prayed: and the fire of his charity took a surplus of ardor from his meditation (M9).

S aint Dominic was a great walker. He undoubtedly spent as much time on the road as he did in the midst of his brothers. He spent a great amount of time traveling; a historian once calculated that he could go up to thirty-two miles in a day. That is a great deal! For that, he had to have much energy as well as time. Dominic used this time for prayer.

It is not a negligible aspect of his prayer to speak of it as itinerant. For Saint Dominic, the route would have been a privileged place where his strength of soul manifested itself, his spirit of mortification, his love for contemplation, and his zeal for preaching. The route would have truly been his cloister, an open cloister, a cloister for prayer while traveling the world.

Brother Buonviso gave us numerous details about Dominic's voyages as he was often his traveling companion. He tells us that Dominic often walked barefoot:

During the trip that took them to Rome, when they left a city, a village or a town, the blessed Brother Dominic would remove his shoes and walk barefoot, carrying his shoes over his shoulder. He would go along like this until they reached another city, village, or town. Then, he would put them back on, but when they left, he would once again remove them (VIE, p. 48).

The same brother also tells us that they, at times, even walked in the driving rain. And Brother Dominic always displayed such happiness and "blessed the Lord by singing, in a loud voice, (...) Ave Maria Stella. When he finished this hymn, he began the Veni Creator, and he continued it to the end, always singing in a loud voice." Since the brother was very admiring, from his comments, we could discern that he would have preferred to have taken cover and waited for the rain to pass. Not everyone is Saint Dominic!

During his travels, Dominic and his companions asked for hospitality from others, be it from some of their brothers, other religious, or whatever they could manage. Dominic always showed himself to be very docile, either to the brothers, or under various circumstances; he followed the will of others and used each opportunity to proclaim the gospel and praise the Lord (see VIE, pp. 36, 49).

We must not believe that these were trips for pleasure; they were just the contrary, true trials. We know that the brothers increased their admiration for their founder when they discovered what these trips represented in terms of the conditions that were present. At times, Dominic reached the very end of his strength, but he always kept some energy to settle the current business and to go pray with the brothers or alone at night.

Dominic was on a perpetual pilgrimage on the road. There was not only continuous prayer, preaching, and fraternal charity, but also poverty there. For in that era, just like today, speed and wealth are connected. Dominic resolutely chose the destitution that he learned from his master, Bishop Diego of Osma. He would always be faithful to it and to such an extent that his health suffered. If he didn't die while on the road, it was almost as if he did, for he was so exhausted when he arrived in Bologna that he had no strength to leave. In a way, we could say that he died on the road—an admirable destiny for an apostle of his caliber and holiness.

His biographer, Jourdain of Saxe, spoke of "his life of travels" (LIB, no. 92) which ended in Bologna. In effect, it was as if Dominic had never stopped walking from the time he left his chapter in Osma (as a youth) until he died. At the beginning, he walked to go to bring the Good News to those who needed it. Then, he walked from one city to another to implant his order.

At the end of his life, considering that his principal ministry was to organize and comfort the brothers he had sent out into the world, he went from one to another, filled with concern for each of them.

Even if he couldn't realize the project that he carried in his heart as a tenacious desire—to go and evangelize the pagans of central Europe, to seek salvation for their souls (see VIE, pp. 43 and 58)—he persuaded others (Brothers Guillaume and Rodolphe) to carry this out.

Brother Dominic couldn't carry this out himself, but his order would always go beyond any and all borders of the world to unite with those who had not yet heard it. In as much as this work will never be finished, the sons of Saint Dominic will travel the routes, praying to their father founder to give them his courage and perseverance.

REFLECTION QUESTIONS

When I travel, am I aware of the opportunities I have to share my faith and spread God's love with others? How do I engage strangers when I deal with them? Am I kind and generous, do I serve strangers and love them as God would want me to? Or am I fearful of and unfeeling toward those people I do not know and who might be different than me? Doesn't God's love bridge all of these chasms that man has created? Am I not God's instrument of peace, and am I not called to bring God's loving message to *all* those I encounter, regardless of my prejudices and opinions?

DAY FOURTEEN

A Man of the Church

FOCUS POINT

Saint Dominic lived in the community of brothers that made up his order. But he also lived in the larger community of the Church, and he felt the powerful familial and mystical ties that make up this great community. Dominic recognized the Church as a family, with everyone a child of God. He also knew the Church as the Mystical Body of Christ, with each person a member of that Body, and Christ as its Head. Dominic knew the Church to be more than an earthly institution, rooted so deeply in heaven as to make it far greater than simply an organization of human invention.

Brother Dominic joined the bishop, and the two of them went to the Council to pray together, with one heart, that the Lord Pope Innocent would confirm, for Brother Dominic and his companions, an order that would come to be and be called the Preachers. They also asked for confirmation for revenue to be assigned to the brothers by the count and the bishop (LIB, no. 40).

S aint Dominic's work and his preaching are resolutely situated "in the middle of the Church," in *medio ecclesiae*, like the Gregorian antiphony is sung in its feast. The preaching of the brothers preachers is not a personal thing. It is *apostolic*, that is, founded on the preaching of the apostles and, therefore, in communion with the successors of the apostles, themselves in communion with the successor of Peter, the pope. Dominic's method was unequivocal. It was in the Church. It was in service to the Church. It spoke in the name of the Church.

From the beginning, he acted in communion with the bishop of Toulouse. And the bishop manifested his agreement by granting Dominic the means to live:

Bishop Foulques of Toulouse, of happy memory, had a tender spot for Brother Dominic, who was loved by man and God, by seeing the regularity of the brothers, their grace and fervor in preaching, was carried away with happiness by this dawn of new light. With the consent of his chapter, he gave them one sixth of the tithes of the diocese, so that, with this revenue, they could get what they needed to live and study (LIB, no. 39).

And it was this same bishop who would give Dominic and his brothers their first church for preaching:

> In the year of the Lord 1216, during the summer, the brothers received, as a donation, their first church in Toulouse, dedicated to Saint Romanus (LIB, no. 44).

Wasn't it amazing to see the bishop of Toulouse take Brother Dominic with him when he went to the Council that was held in Rome? There, Dominic would make profound and long-lasting connections with many members of the Roman Curia, in particular with the bishop of Ostie, who would soon become Pope Honorius III, succeeding Pope Innocent III. It would be he who would give the order their definitive confirmation.

Dominic attached the greatest importance to his connections. It wasn't for him to place himself in the Roman machine, but to be in real communion with Christ's Church. For the one who preaches the gospel without following in the authentic tradition of the apostles exposes himself to be preaching for himself and in error. Also, the Constitutions of the order insisted on this connection on numerous occasions, which is also a responsibility.

> We consecrate ourselves completely to God through the profession which we incorporate into our order and we dedicate ourselves to the Church in a new way....
>
> Having chosen the mission of the apostles, we also assume their life....
>
> In our aspect as co-operators with the order of bishops... (LCO, fundamental constitution, § 3, 4, 5).

The Order of Friars Preachers, following and in the spirit of their founder, consider their life to be completely consecrated to the service of the Church of Christ. If, like Saint Paul, they hope, in the end, to get something personal from their preaching, it is not primarily for themselves that they are working. Their ministry is the one that Christ entrusted to the Church: the salvation of souls. They treat their prayer as an office, that is, a true responsibility that one must assume through perseverance and faithfulness, in service to the Church and all of the intentions that it presents to the Lord. Thus, their entire life becomes an ecclesiastical life, that is what is implied by the great responsibilities which have been entrusted to them.

Right from the first years of the order, there was an image that expressed this mission that Saint Dominic and his brothers had received from the Church.

When the man of God, Dominic, was in Rome and praying, in the presence of God in the basilica of Saint Peter, for the preservation and development of the order that the divine right hand propagated through his concerns, God's hand came down upon him. He saw Peter and Paul, these princes full of glory appear. The first, Peter, entrusted him with a cane; Paul, a book; and the two of them added: "Go out and preach, for God has chosen you for this ministry." Then, in an instant, he seemed to see his sons dispersed throughout the entire world, going two by two, preaching the Word of God to the people (EVA, pp. 86–87).

The image speaks for itself. It expresses this vital connection with the Church: Saint Dominic, as is his usual habit, is praying. That day, he was praying in a significant place: in that basilica in Rome that was erected on the tombs of the martyrs; there, where all Christians go to revive their faith at the very source of Tradition. He prayed for the order that he was in the process of founding, an order that would have for its mission the prolongation of the actions of the apostles. In his prayer, there came the figures of the two columns upon which the Church rests: Peter and Paul. Dominic felt as if he was seized by their charisma and comforted in his intuitions; that is what the two insignias of the itinerant preachers mean: a cane and a book, accompanied by the evangelical precept to go and preach. For Saint Dominic, he knew no other preaching than the one he lived in communion with the Church. Thus, we read in the papal bull of confirmation of the order by Pope Honorius III: "we place (them) under the protection of the blessed Peter and our church in Toulouse" (VIE, p. 152).

We always err with respect to the Church when we analyze it according to sociological criteria. Its true nature is beyond human consideration. The Church participates in the mystery of Jesus himself. In the same way that he is both a true God and a true man, the reality of the Church is divine as well as human. The Church assures the world this real and hidden presence that God assured in Jesus during his earthly life. To be cut off from the Church to be cut off from the Mystical Body of Christ, that is, to be outside of Christ. Saint Dominic's love for Christ is, therefore, absolutely inseparable from his love for the Church. It goes without saying.

In the chronicles of Saint Dominic's life, we don't find any long discourses about this theme of attachment to the Church. The question doesn't even have to be asked. Dominic lived in the Church like he lived in a family. He was attached to it with a vital connection. It was from the Church that he received life and it's completely natural that he gave himself to it in service.

But his attachment was not automatic. Remaining completely faithful, he reached a new method in his way of serving the Church.

Thus, at the beginning of his career, he naturally followed the papal legates. But rapidly, and in connection with the bishop from his home diocese, Diego of Osma, he left his official missions in order to dedicate himself to direct contact with people. Then, through time, seeing the importance of organizing this direct kind of preaching, he created this permanent mission of preaching that would become his Order of Friars Preachers, which he gave in service to the Church. Thus, his fidelity was inventive. And for himself, Dominic testified that it manifested the profound unity of his life. From the most intimate of his sparks of prayer all the way to his most institutional decisions, he lived in communion with Christ, and with the Church of Christ.

Someone who wants to follow in Dominic's footsteps must take a close look at his attachment to the Church, at what impact it has on him, at his behavior in the ecclesiastical community, and, finally, at the unity of his life.

REFLECTION QUESTIONS

What do I see as my part in the Church? Do I feel like a part of the Mystical Body described above? Do I see the Church as a family-centered entity? How do I relate to the other members of this family? Do I make an attempt to reach out to them, to welcome them, to be welcomed by them? How might I take it upon myself to help draw my local parish family closer together? When I am feeling distant from God and my fellow brother and sisters, do I pray that the Church will energize and renew my tired state?

DAY FIFTEEN

A Man, a Brother, a Father

FOCUS POINT

Saint Dominic, like all of us, was seen in different roles by the many people in his life. To some, he was a fellow brother in the Dominican order; to others, he was a spiritual adviser of great assistance; and to others still, he was the esteemed founder of a great religious order. Though he was seen differently by varying people, Dominic was, simply, a man of God who was energized to bring God to everyone. From the learned theologians to the children he encountered, Dominic shared the gospel message and God's great love. May we be moved by the Holy Spirit to do the same in our own lives.

My brothers, let us follow, as much as we can, in the footsteps of our father, and at the same time, give thanks to the Redeemer who gave his servants the route they are traveling and a leader of this caliber and, through him, we once again are born to the light of the holy life. And pray to the Father of mercy so that, under the action of the Holy Spirit, we will also be found worthy to reach the same goal of perpetual happiness and eternal bliss into which he has, happily and for all time, entered. Amen! (LIB, no. 109).

This is how Jourdain of Saxe (Dominic's successor) ends his portrayal of the father of the order. This prayer well states the complete attachment that his sisters and brothers have for Saint Dominic. It is the charisma of the true founders that attracts souls with the desire to consecrate themselves to God and to serve along the guidelines given by them. There is a special charm there, which would not hold if it were too human, but which withstands the test of time because it comes from God.

Saint Dominic was blessed with such a radiance which primarily came from the quality of his presence. We could say that his humility was imposed on him, or rather, that it was self-imposed. That is how humility is with the great saints, just like the great thinkers knew to give their knowledge even to children.

Right from our first contact, we felt that Brother Dominic was completely filled with the divine presence, this presence with which he penetrated himself during his long nights of prayer. He was a man inhabited with it. The Holy Spirit dwelled within him. We can't deny feeling it. "His moral perfection and the spark of divine fervor that carried it" (LIB, no. 103) flies out at us, to our hearts, even to those he zealously pursued (heretics) with his pro-active preaching. Just as Jourdain said: "...he infiltrated himself, right from the first gaze, into the affection of everyone" (LIB, no. 103).

His presence was impressive. He touched the hearts of those to whom he spoke. He knew how to listen to them, not as a task or duty, but because he loved them.

What was striking about him were his qualities as a man. The austerity of his life did not alter his beautiful humanity. He was not one of those ascetics that disturb us, who appear as living reproaches. Women found him handsome, they liked his face and his presence. Here is a testimony by Sister Cecile in this regard:

> Here is a portrait of the blessed Dominic: medium height, lean body, handsome face, fair of skin color, hair and beard slightly auburn, beautiful eyes. From his forehead and eyebrow came a sort of shining splendor that attracted the reverence and affection of everyone. He was always smiling and happy, unless he was moved with compassion as a result of an affliction of his neighbor. He had hands that were long and beautiful; a great voice, lovely and harmonious. He was never bald and his crown of hair was complete, peppered with a few sparse white hairs (VIE, p. 124).

Even if time and memory had embellished her portrait of her spiritual father due to her increasing age, Sister Cecile has left us with a strong impression of blossomed humanity.

But if he knew how to be a brother to everyone, Dominic was, above all, a father. The father is the one who engenders. Dominic engendered a multitude of sons and daughters for whom he is neither responsible for their physical life, nor their Christian one, but at least their religious life. All of those who have entered the order know that they are born from the always active prayer of the father of the preachers. Dominic, who wanted this order with all of the strength of his soul, continues to want it from on high in heaven, just as Jourdain expresses in this beautiful prayer:

> *O most holy priest of God,*
> *glorious confessor, eminent preacher,*
> *blessed Dominic, man chosen by the Lord,*
> *in your era you had been between every object of*
> *his concern and predilection for your glorious life*
> *through his miracles and his doctrine;*
> *and now, we rejoice to have you near*
> *the Lord God to be our particular intercessor.*
> *It is you I venerate above all other saints,*
> *that I cry out....*
> *(VIE, p. 129).*

Saint Dominic also loved like a father and was loved like a father. When he died, there was a great outpouring of grief like for a father whose loss leaves a great void of affection in a family. Like a father, he gave his sons training that was founded upon values that were as transmitted by example as they were by word. He led the way. He gave them the tone. He stimulated and sanctioned if necessary; in a phrase, he turned his children into well brought up men and women: that is the true quality of a father.

He left them a name, one that is used by his children with great pride: the Dominicans. That family name can also express a connection with the Lord (dominical—referring to Sunday, the Lord's day; also from the Latin *dominicus*, meaning Lord), as well as one with Dominic.

As well as being a founder, Saint Dominic was a patriarch in the sense that he was the origin of a multitude of families, just as the father of a large family has many sons and daughters who, in their turn, have families, and so forth. The connection between all of these families is the patriarch. It is from him that life flows, it is transmitted in the same way as is his name and his spirit.

On the feast day of the order, November 7, the following letter, from Jourdain of Saxe, addressed to the brothers, is read during the Liturgy of the Hours. With it, we end these fifteen days of prayer with Saint Dominic:

> To my very dear brothers in Christ! I pray for you and warn you with all my strength, beseeching you through the One who redeemed you with his divine blood and gave you life through his death: do not forget your profession, nor your life's project. Remember your predecessors...one of them surpasses all the others: our venerable father and of holy memory, Dominic; when he lived amongst us in the flesh, he conducted himself according to the spirit. Not content to not fulfill the desires of the flesh, he strangled them. In his nourishment, clothes, and way of living, he manifested true poverty. Endlessly, in prayer, specially compassionate, he was quick to shed tears for his children, that is, he burned with zeal for souls. He did not collapse under difficulties, he quietly withstood opposition.
>
> His works tell us, and his virtues and miracles attest to, the stature he rose to on earth in our midst. The stature to which he will dwell, next to God, has been

manifested by signs and proven by miracles, in these last days, when we have transferred his sacred body from his first tomb to a more honorable one.

We must, then, praise him to our Redeemer, the Son of God, Jesus Christ, who has deemed to choose such a servant and put him as our leader like our father in order to shape us, through his institution of an ordinary regular life and inflame us through the example of his bursting holiness (in the *Proper of the Order of Friars Preachers*, Liturgy of the Hours, sanctorum, Paris, 1983, p. 398).

REFLECTION QUESTIONS

In what different capacities do I serve God in my life? As father, brother, mother, sister, adviser, "sounding board," friend, spiritual director, son, or daughter? Do I recognize that, although I may approach each of these roles differently, I am still the same person at the center, a person who is loved by God and who is called to spread God's Word and share his love? At the conclusion of these fifteen days of prayer with Saint Dominic, what aspect(s) of this great saint's personality do I most admire and seek to incorporate in my own life? Might I pray for the intercession of Saint Dominic in this regard?

Bibliography

Auth, Charles R. *A Dominican Bibliography and Book of Reference, 1216–1992: A List of Works in English by and about Members of the Order of Friars Preachers, Founded by St. Dominic de Guzman (c. 1171–1221) and Confirmed by Pope Honorius III, December 22, 1216.* Peter Lang Publishing, 2000.

Bedouelle, Guy. *In the Image of Saint Dominic: Nine Portraits of Dominican Life.* Ignatius Press, 1994.

———. *Saint Dominic: The Grace of the Word.* Ignatius Press, 1987.

Beebe, Catherine. *Saint Dominic and the Rosary.* Ignatius Press, 1996.

Brady, Gerard K. *Saint Dominic: Pilgrim of Light.* Burns and Oates, 1957.

Jarrett, Bede. *Life of Saint Dominic.* Image Books, 1964.

Monshau, Michael. *Praying With Dominic.* Koch, Carl, ed. St. Mary's Press, 1995.

Woods, Richard. *Mysticism and Prophecy: The Dominican Tradition (Traditions of Christian Spirituality).* Orbis Books, 1998.